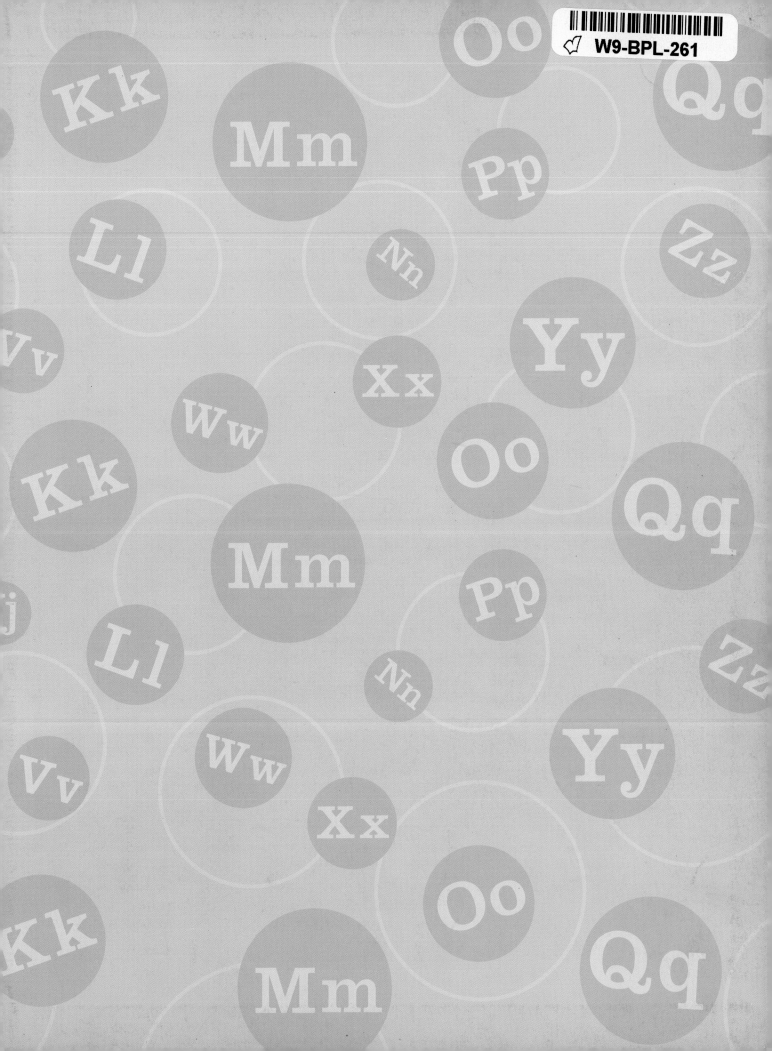

Nickelodeon, Nickelodeon All Grown Up, Nickelodeon Rocket Power, The Adventures of Jimmy
Neutron: Boy Genius, As Told by Ginger Foutley, CatDog, Danny Phantom, The Fairly OddParents,
Hey Arnold!, Rugrats, SpongeBob SquarePants, The Wild Thornberrys, and all related titles,
logos, and characters are trademarks of Viacom International, Inc. Nickelodeon All Grown
Up, Nickelodeon Rocket Power, As Told by Ginger Foutley, Rugrats, and The Wild
Thornberrys created by Klasky Csupo, Inc. CatDog created by Peter Hannan. Hey Arnold!
created by Craig Bartlett. The Fairly OddParents and Danny Phantom created by Butch Hartman.
SpongeBob SquarePants created by Stephen Hillenburg.

Book design by Jessica Dacher.
Typeset in Trade Gothic, Clarendon and Sign Painter.
Manufactured in China.

ISBN 0-8118-4953-8

Distributed in Canada by Raincoast Books
9050 Shaughnessy Street, Vancouver, British Columbia V6P 6E5

10 9 8 7 6 5 4 3 2 1

Chronicle Books LLC
85 Second Street, San Francisco, California 94105

www.chroniclebooks.com • www.nick.com

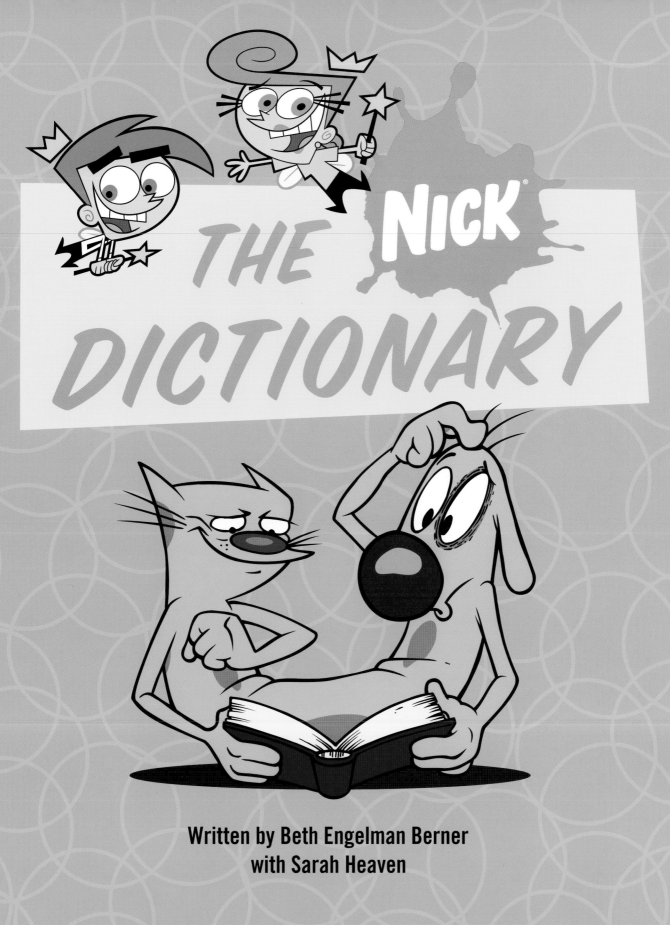

THE NICK DICTIONARY

Written by Beth Engelman Berner
with Sarah Heaven

chronicle books · san francisco

A NOTE TO PARENTS

WELCOME YOUR CHILD TO THE WORLD OF WORDS! JOIN SPONGEBOB, JIMMY, WANDA, AND ALL YOUR CHILD'S FAVORITE NICKELODEON CHARACTERS AS THEY INTRODUCE HUNDREDS OF HIGH-INTEREST VOCABULARY WORDS.

KID-CENTRIC APPROACH TO LEARNING

The Nick Dictionary will help foster a love of learning as your child expands vocabulary and builds valuable reading-readiness skills. Each word has been carefully chosen by educators, representing both the words children encounter every day and new vocabulary that will intrigue young learners. Definitions are straightforward and expressed in clear, concise language. Sentences that use the words in context, along with engaging illustrations, further enhance each definition by making even the most abstract concepts easy to understand. After all, it's hard to forget what *full* means after they have seen Patrick's mouth full of snow!

USING THIS DICTIONARY

We recommend that you use this dictionary as a reference guide, wordbook, storybook, and game. Encourage your child to flip through the pages and delight in the illustrations, or help them look up words they would like to learn. Experiment with rhyming, guessing, and categorizing games to add new dimensions to learning vocabulary. Refer to pages 8–13 for helpful language-learning information to share with your child.

WITH *THE NICK DICTIONARY*, LEARNING BECOMES PLAYFUL AND ENTERTAINING!

HOW TO LOOK UP A WORD

There are nearly 1,000 words in this dictionary. That's a lot of words, so it's helpful to know a few things about how to use a dictionary.

The words in a dictionary are in alphabetical order. This means that the words are listed in the same order as the letters of the alphabet. So words that start with the letter *A* come first, then words that start with the letter *B,* and so on. To help you remember the order of the alphabet, the alphabet is printed across the top of the pages.

To look up a word,
1. Start by thinking of what letter the word starts with. For example, the word *bake* starts with a *B.*
2. Turn to the beginning of the section that lists the words that start with *B.*
3. Think of the next letter of the word. For *bake,* the next letter after *B* is *A.*
4. Look through all the words that start with "ba" until you find the word *bake.*

NOW YOU TRY!

WORD CHALLENGE

Let's practice! On a sheet of paper, write these words in alphabetical order. Find them in the dictionary to see if you are right.

banana   *violin*   *machine*   *tail*   *newspaper*

These words begin with the same letter, so take a close look at their second letters to put them in alphabetical order.

feather   *family*   *flashlight*   *furniture*   *four*

You'll need to look at the third letter in each word to put these words in order!

wave   *warm*   *wake*   *watch*   *wash*

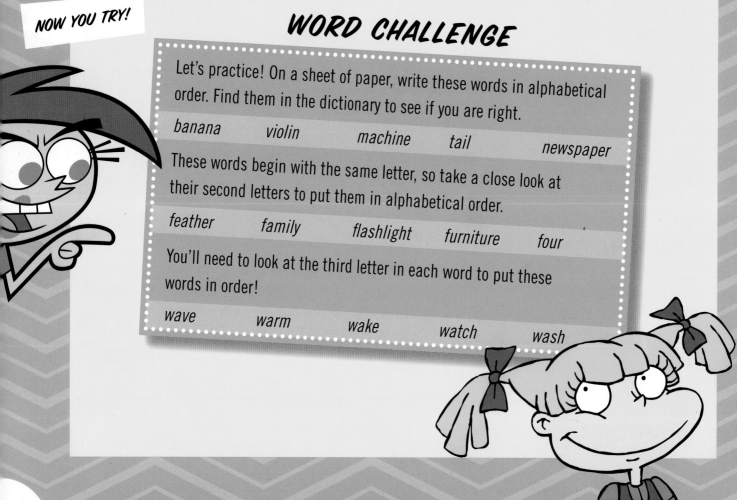

6

ALL KINDS OF WORDS

Just as people do different types of jobs, words do different jobs, too. Some words tell us the names of things. Other words tell us what action is taking place. Still other words describe things. All these kinds of words and more can be found in this dictionary. Each different kind of word has a special name.

NOUNS

A noun is a word that names a person, place, or thing. The words *doctor* (a person), *school* (a place), and *toy* (a thing) are all nouns. Words like *month, imagination,* and *idea* are nouns too because they are things, even though you cannot see or touch them. To tell if a word is a noun ask yourself, "Is this word a person, place, or thing?"

WORD CHALLENGE

Find the noun in each sentence. (Looking up the word in the dictionary will tell you if you guessed correctly.) Some of the sentences have more than one noun, so try to spot them all!

1. The airplane flies fast.
2. There are lots of books at school.
3. Marbles come in all different colors.

BASKETBALL *IS A NOUN!*

VERBS

A verb is a word that tells what someone or something is doing. For example, in the sentence "Debbie reads a book," *reads* is the verb because it tells what Debbie is doing. Because they show action, verbs are also known as "action words." Even *sleep* and *think* are action words, even though there's not much action going on when you do them!

WORD CHALLENGE

In each list of words below, one word is a verb. The rest are nouns. Can you identify the verb in each list?

guitar, chase, pineapple, football
bed, dinosaur, see, jack-o'-lantern
hide, sandbox, window, eyeglasses

RUN *IS A VERB TOO!*

ADJECTIVES

An adjective is a word that describes a person, place, or thing. In other words, adjectives describe nouns! If we say "Jimmy Neutron makes great inventions," *inventions* is the noun and *great* is the adjective that describes it.

WORD CHALLENGE

The words *slow, funny, small* and *lazy* are all adjectives. Choose the adjective that best describes each of the Nickelodeon characters below. One has been done for you.

slow   SpongeBob

funny   Patrick

small   Gary

lazy   Plankton

Most words in this book are nouns, verbs, and adjectives. But there are a few other types of words in this book as well:

ADVERBS

An adverb generally describes an action. It can tell you when (like the word *now*), where (like the word *outside*), or how (like the word *backward*) an action takes place.

BACKWARD *IS AN ADVERB.*

PREPOSITIONS

A preposition often tells *where* someone or something is. In the sentence "SpongeBob feels a little squashed when he is trapped under Patrick," the preposition *under* describes where SpongeBob is. For more examples of how prepositions are used to describe a person or thing's position, look up these words in your dictionary:

above   *behind*   *below*   *in*   *on*

INTERJECTIONS

An interjection can help show emotion. Look for this interjection in your dictionary: *Yippee!*

EEEEEEEEEK!

MAKING WORD CONNECTIONS

PLURAL NOUNS

A noun that is more than one person, place, or thing is a *plural* noun. To talk about more than one of a noun, we often add *-s, -es,* or *-ies* to the end of the word:

teacher ⟶ *teachers*   *box* ⟶ *boxes*   *family* ⟶ *families*

When some nouns become plural, their spelling changes a lot. For example, one *mouse,* two *mice.* When you look up different nouns, try making them plural.

VERB TENSES

Look at the sentences below.

*SpongeBob **holds** on to his skateboard.*
*SpongeBob is **holding** on to his skateboard.*
*SpongeBob **held** on to his skateboard.*
*SpongeBob **will hold** on to his skateboard.*

HOLD ON, SPONGEBOB!

The way the word *hold* appears in a sentence changes depending on whether the action takes place in the present, past, or future. As you read about different verbs, make up sentences that use the words in the present, past, and future and see how the word changes.

WORDS THAT ARE OPPOSITES

Many words in this dictionary have an antonym, or a word that means the exact opposite. For example, the opposite of *happy* is *sad*. For many words in this dictionary that have opposites, the antonym is identified in the definition.

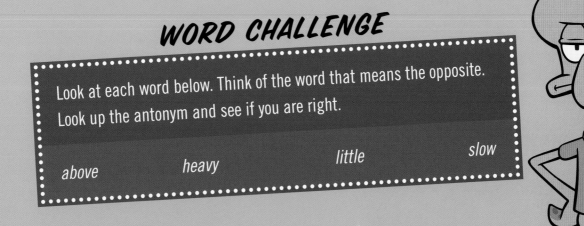

WORD CHALLENGE

Look at each word below. Think of the word that means the opposite. Look up the antonym and see if you are right.

| above | heavy | little | slow |

SAME SOUND, DIFFERENT MEANING

There are many words that sound alike but have different meanings and different spellings. These words are known as homophones. The words *sea* and *see, weak* and *week,* and *right* and *write* are some of the homophones in this book. What are some other homophones?

WACKY, WONDERFUL WORDS

Did you know that a word can have more than one meaning? For example, the word *bat* is both a flying animal and a stick for hitting a baseball!

A word can also be used in more than one way, for example, as a verb or as a noun. Think about the word *hug*. In the sentence, "SpongeBob and Patrick hug each other," *hug* is a verb. In the sentence, "SpongeBob gives Patrick a hug," *hug* is a noun!

To keep things simple, this dictionary generally gives only one meaning for each word. And it labels each word only one way (such as noun *or* verb), even though a word could possibly be used in other ways too. So as you look up words in this dictionary, think about whether they may have other meanings and other ways of being used in a sentence. You may be surprised!

HAPPY!

SAD

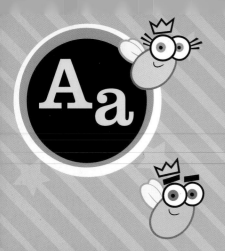

Above *preposition*
On top of or higher up than something else. *Above* is the opposite of *below*.

Wanda flies above Cosmo.

Across *preposition*
From one side to the other.

Chester has braces across his teeth.

Accordion *noun*
A musical instrument with a keyboard at each end and an area for pushing air in the middle.

Squidward plays the trumpet and the accordion at the same time.

Actor *noun*
A person who acts in plays or movies or on TV.

When you are an actor on the Bikini Bottom Broadway stage, you get to sing, dance, and talk into the microphone.

2 + 2 = 4

Add *verb*
To combine numbers to make a bigger number. *Add* is the opposite of *subtract*.

When you add two plus two, you get four.

Acorn *noun*
The nut that grows on an oak tree.

Eddie's mouth is full of acorns.

Adjective *noun*
A word that describes a person, place, or thing.

Short is an adjective, and so is tall.

tall

short

Adult *noun*
A grown-up.

*Jimmy Neutron's dad, Hugh, is an **adult**. When Jimmy grows up, he'll be one, too.*

Alarm clock *noun*
A clock you can set to wake you up at a certain time with music or a sound.

*What time do you set your **alarm clock** to get up for school?*

Adventure *noun*
Something you do that is exciting or different.

*For Eliza, helping her animal friends is always an **adventure**.*

Alike *adjective*
The same in some way. *Alike* is the opposite of *different*.

*The three dogs look **alike**.*

After *preposition*
Later than, or behind someone or something in order. *After* is the opposite of *before*.

*A ghost chases **after** the man.*

Alphabet *noun*
A list of all the letters used to write words.

*There are 26 letters in the **alphabet**.*

Airplane *noun*
A winged flying vehicle powered by an engine.

*An **airplane** is heavier than air, but its powerful engine makes it fly.*

Ambulance *noun*

A van used to bring sick or injured people to a hospital.

*The lights of the **ambulance** flash to let people know to get out of its way.*

Animation *noun*

A way of making drawings seem to move, act, and speak.

*This Ultra Lord video is Sheen's favorite cartoon **animation**.*

Anchor *noun*

A heavy piece of metal attached to a boat to keep it from floating away.

*The pointy ends of the **anchor** help it dig into the ocean floor.*

Animal *noun*

A living thing that is not a plant.

*Humans are **animals**, just like zebras, antelopes, and turtles.*

Answer *noun*

The solution to a problem, or a response to a question.

*Books can be useful for finding an **answer** to a question.*

Anteater *noun*

A four-legged, long-nosed animal that eats ants by sucking them up with its tongue.

*The **anteater** is often found in rain forests.*

Appear *verb*
To come into view. *Appear* is the opposite of *disappear.*

*Cosmo uses his magic to make superheroes **appear**.*

Archery *noun*
A sport where a bow is used to shoot arrows at a target.

*You score points in **archery** by getting your arrow as close to the center of the target as possible.*

Armadillo *noun*
A short, four-legged animal with an armor of bony plates.

*The hard shell on this **armadillo** will protect it from other animals.*

Apple *noun*
A round fruit with red, yellow, or green skin.

*Eating an **apple** a day helps your teeth and body stay healthy and strong.*

Arrow *noun*
A thin, pointy stick shot into the air with a bow.

*It looks like cupid Tommy's **arrow** could unclog a toilet.*

Aquarium *noun*
A tank of water where sea creatures and plants can live.

*When Cosmo and Wanda turn into goldfish, they live in an **aquarium**.*

Artichoke *noun*
A green vegetable with tightly packed leaves and a soft center.

*When you eat an **artichoke**, you peel away its leaves until you get to the best part, called the heart.*

Artist *noun*
A person who makes art, such as paintings, sculptures, music, or poems.

*Squidward is an **artist** who paints self-portraits.*

Athlete *noun*
A person who takes part in exercise, sports, or other physical games.

*Reggie is a good **athlete**.*

Ask *verb*
To say something in the form of a question, or to request a response.

*Brad would like to **ask** a question.*

Audience *noun*
A group of people gathered together to watch a play, concert, movie, or other performance.

*SpongeBob sits in the **audience** and watches a movie.*

Astronaut *noun*
A person who travels in space to learn about the universe beyond Earth.

*This **astronaut** may have just spotted an alien!*

Ax *noun*
A tool with a long, thick handle and a sharp blade.

*An **ax** is often used to chop wood.*

Baby *noun*
A very young child.

*As a **baby**, Dil liked to eat, sleep, and play with his pacifier.*

Badminton *noun*
A sport where two or more players use rackets to hit a game piece called a shuttlecock back and forth over a net.

Badminton is similar to tennis, but you use a shuttlecock instead of a ball.

Bb

Babysit *verb*
To take care of children for a short time while their parents are away.

*Vicky may **babysit** Timmy, but that doesn't mean she likes it!*

Bag *noun*
A pouch or sack used to hold or carry things.

*Wanda and Cosmo have turned into **bags**!*

Backpack *noun*
A bag with two straps that go over your shoulders.

*Macie's **backpack** is full of books.*

KISS THE COOK

Backward *adverb*
In the direction behind you as you face forward.

*Reggie is skating **backward**.*

Bake *verb*
To cook something in the oven.

*Squidward likes to **bake** not-so-delicious cakes.*

Balance *verb*
To keep yourself steady so you do not tip over.

*Can SpongeBob **balance** himself without falling down?*

Banana *noun*
A long, yellow fruit that has to be peeled before eating.

*A **banana** is soft and easy to chew.*

Ball *noun*
A round object used for games or sports.

*A big, inflatable **ball** is great to take to the beach.*

Ballet *noun*
A kind of dance that often tells a story.

*Angelica's **ballet** is called Angelica's Lake!*

Band *noun*
A group of musicians who play together.

*In the Jellyfish Jam **Band**, Patrick plays the drums. Rock on!*

Balloon *noun*
A rubber bag that can be filled with air or helium.

*Carl's **balloon** is shaped like a bat.*

Bandage *noun*
A strip of fabric used to protect a wound until it heals.

*Patrick is all wrapped up in a **bandage**.*

20

Bank *noun*
A place where people keep their money.

*Mr. Krabs has so much money, he should put it in a **bank**.*

Basketball *noun*
A game in which two teams try to toss a ball through a hoop and prevent their opponents from doing the same.

*Reggie and Twister are playing **basketball**.*

Baseball *noun*
A game in which two teams take turns batting and catching a ball.

*SpongeBob loves to play **baseball**.*

Bat *noun*
A winged animal that sleeps during the day and flies about at night.

*A **bat** sleeps upside down.*

Basket *noun*
A container made out of straw that has been woven together.

*A **basket** is perfect when you are going on a picnic because it is light to carry but very strong.*

Bath *noun*
A way of cleaning yourself by sitting in a tub of water and washing your body.

*When SpongeBob takes a **bath**, his body gets clean, and his floor does, too!*

21

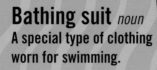

Bathing suit *noun*
A special type of clothing worn for swimming.

Bathing suits *are made of special quick-drying fabric.*

Bed *noun*
A piece of furniture you lie on to sleep or rest.

*Jimmy has a very unusual **bed!***

Beach *noun*
A sandy or pebbly shore along a lake or ocean.

*Timmy, Wanda, and Cosmo play in the waves at the **beach**.*

Bee *noun*
An insect with four wings that makes honey.

*The **bee** protects itself by stinging with its stinger.*

Beak *noun*
The hard, pointy mouth on a bird.

*This bird's **beak** is long and thin.*

Beehive *noun*
A nest in which bees live and make honey.

*Bees don't like it when you disturb their **beehive**.*

Bear *noun*
A large, heavy animal with shaggy hair and a small tail.

*Black bears and polar bears are the most well-known types of **bear**.*

Beetle *noun*
A flying insect with four wings.

*A **beetle** has two pairs of wings. The hard wings on top protect the soft wings underneath.*

Before *preposition*
Earlier than, or in front of someone or something in order. *Before* is the opposite of *after.*

Before Patrick lies in the sun, he puts on sunscreen.

Bell *noun*
An instrument that makes a ringing sound when it is struck.

Bells make different sounds depending on their shape and size.

Below *preposition*
Under or lower than something. *Below* is the opposite of *above.*

Tommy stands *below* Dil.

Begin *verb*
To start something. *Begin* is the opposite of *end.*

Timmy is about to *begin* his speech.

Belt *noun*
A strap worn around your waist.

Timmy's dad keeps his pants up with a black *belt.*

Behind *preposition*
In back of something.

Gary hides *behind* SpongeBob.

Bench *noun*
A long seat for two or more people.

Arnold sits on the red *bench,* waiting for the bus.

23

Bend *verb*
To curve.

*Reggie must **bend** low for this pose.*

Big *adjective*
Large. ***Big*** is the opposite of ***little***.

*The tires on SpongeBob's monster boat-truck are **big**.*

Beside *preposition*
Next to.

*Tommy dances **beside** the pumpkin.*

Binoculars *noun*
Two small telescopes joined together that let you see things that are far away.

*When you look through **binoculars**, everything looks bigger and closer.*

Between *preposition*
In the middle of.

*Goddard is **between** Jimmy and Carl.*

Birthday *noun*
The date you were born.

*When is your **birthday**?*

Bicycle *noun*
A vehicle with two wheels, two handlebars, and a seat, plus pedals you turn with your feet to make it move.

*The **bicycle** is green.*

Bite *verb*
To cut into something with your teeth.

*SpongeBob can't wait to **bite** into his Krabby Patty!*

Blow verb
To push your breath out of your mouth.

*Kimi likes to **blow** on a dandelion and make a wish.*

Book noun
Pieces of paper joined together and attached inside a cover.

*Debbie likes to read a good **book**.*

Boat noun
A vehicle that floats on water.

*This **boat** has a big sail to help it move.*

Boomerang noun
A curved stick that comes back to you when you throw it.

*A **boomerang** is often made of wood.*

Body noun
The entire form of a shape or thing.

*Name all the parts of Crimson Chin's **body**.*

HEAD

NECK

SHOULDER

ARM

HAND

KNEE

LEG

FOOT

Boots noun
Tall shoes that cover your feet and part of your ankles or legs.

***Boots** like these help protect firefighters from heat and water.*

Borrow verb
To use something for a while and then give it back.

*Patrick **borrows** ornaments from his Christmas tree.*

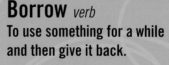

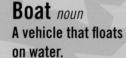

Bouquet *noun*
A bunch of flowers gathered together.

*These roses are arranged in a **bouquet**.*

Boy *noun*
A child who is not a girl.

*Timmy is a ten-year-old **boy**.*

Bowl *noun*
A rounded dish that holds food.

*This **bowl** is filled with buttery popcorn.*

Bracelet *noun*
A band or chain worn around your wrist.

*Angelica's pink **bracelet** matches her watch.*

Bowling *noun*
A game you play by rolling a heavy ball to knock pins down.

*SpongeBob likes **bowling**, but he's not very good at it.*

Brave *adjective*
Feeling afraid to do something but willing to do it anyway.

*Cleft always acts **brave**, even when he's scared.*

Box *noun*
A square container used to hold things.

*What's in the **box**, Patrick?*

Breakfast *noun*
The first meal of the day.

Breakfast gives you energy to start your day.

Brother *noun*
A boy who has the same parents as someone else.

Brad is Tuck's brother.

Breathe *verb*
To take air in and out through your mouth and nose.

When it's cold outside, you can see your breath when you breathe.

Bring *verb*
To take something along.

Gerald remembers to bring his books to school.

Brush *noun*
A tool with a handle and bristles.

A brush can come in any shape or size.

Broccoli *noun*
A vegetable with stalks and green or purple flowered heads.

The tops of broccoli are called florets.

Bubble *noun*
A thin, light film of liquid filled with air.

Do you know how to blow a bubble?

27

Bug *noun*
An insect or other tiny animal.

*This **bug** has a hard covering to protect it.*

Bush *noun*
A large plant with many leaves and branches.

*Eliza and Darwin are hiding behind the **bush**. Do you think they notice the large lion behind them?*

Build *verb*
To put something together.

*Dil **builds** a baby snowman!*

Bull *noun*
A male cow.

*One time Francis turned into a **bull**!*

Butter *noun*
A yellow food made from milk.

***Butter** is often served on a special dish.*

Bus *noun*
A large vehicle that carries people from place to place.

*This **bus** can carry a lot of people.*

Butterfly *noun*
An insect with four large wings.

*A **butterfly** landed on Kimi's finger.*

Button *noun*
A small knob or disk used to fasten clothes together.

*Dil's parents have to undo each **button** on his clothes when it's diaper-changing time.*

Cake *noun*
A sweet dessert usually made with flour and sugar.

*Which **cake** do you think tastes better?*

FRUITCAKE

Calculator *noun*
A machine that can add, subtract, divide, and multiply numbers.

*Who said using a **calculator** makes math problems easier?*

Call *verb*
To use the phone to speak with someone who is in a different place.

*Patrick is trying to **call** his best pal, Spongebob.*

Camel *noun*
A large animal that lives in the desert.

*This **camel** has one hump but some camels have two.*

Camera *noun*
A machine that takes pictures.

*Taking pictures with a **camera** helps you remember interesting sights and events.*

29

Camp verb
To sleep outdoors in a tent.

*Debbie has all the things she needs to **camp**, except someone else to carry her backpack.*

Cape noun
A coat without sleeves that fastens at the neck.

*When the Bronze Kneecap runs, his **cape** flaps in the wind.*

Cc

Candle noun
A piece of wax with a string inside that is burned to give off light.

*A lighted **candle** decorates this birthday cupcake.*

Canoe noun
A long, narrow boat that you use paddles with to move through water.

*Angelica enjoys the scenery while Chuckie paddles their **canoe**.*

REPORT CARD

Card noun
A thick, often folded, piece of paper with a note written on it that is given to someone.

*Uh-oh! Arnold is unhappy with his report **card**.*

Cantaloupe noun
A round fruit that is a type of melon.

*The inside of a **cantaloupe** is sweet and juicy.*

Carrot noun
A long, orange vegetable.

*A **carrot** can be eaten raw, cooked, or even baked in a cake!*

Carry *verb*
To hold something and take it from one place to another.

*You can use your glove to **carry** a baseball.*

Cauliflower *noun*
A white vegetable with stalks and flowered heads.

*You can cook **cauliflower** or eat it raw.*

Cartoon *noun*
A movie or TV show that uses drawings instead of live actors.

*Cat likes watching a funny **cartoon**, while Dog prefers watching a sad movie.*

Cello *noun*
A musical instrument that looks like a large violin and is also played by moving a bow across the strings.

*You can make beautiful music on a **cello**.*

Cat *noun*
A furry pet animal that meows and has sharp teeth and claws.

*This **cat** has soft, white fur and long whiskers.*

Center *noun*
The middle part.

*Wanda is in the **center** of her inner tube.*

THAT'S **SO** ANNOYING!

Century *noun*
One hundred years.

*A **century** ago, most women did not wear jeans.*

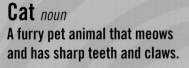

a b **c** d e f g h i j k l m

Catch *verb*
To grab something as it comes near you or moves away.

Catch the ball, Tommy!

Chase *verb*
To go after something.

Danny Phantom chases a ghost.

Cereal *noun*
A breakfast food made of grain or corn.

Cereal tastes good with milk and berries.

Cheese *noun*
A kind of food made from milk.

Swiss cheese is known for its holes.

Chair *noun*
A piece of furniture you sit on.

After a long day at the Krusty Krab, SpongeBob likes to relax in his chair.

Cheetah *noun*
A large, spotted cat.

A cheetah can run faster than any other animal in the world.

Cherry *noun*
A round red or purplish red fruit that grows on a tree.

Cherries have long, thin stems.

Chess *noun*
A two-player game played with game pieces on a checkered board.

*In **chess**, you have to try to capture the other player's king before yours is taken.*

Chimney *noun*
A tall tube through a house that carries smoke from a fireplace to the outside.

*Patrick is stuck in the **chimney**.*

Chew *verb*
To use your teeth to grind something into small pieces.

*After his workout, SpongeBob **chews** a crisp apple.*

Chimpanzee *noun*
A kind of ape with a long, lanky body.

*A **chimpanzee** likes to eat bananas.*

Chocolate *noun*
A food made from cacao beans and usually sweetened.

*This is a bar of **chocolate**.*

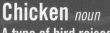

Chicken *noun*
A type of bird raised on a farm for its eggs and meat.

*A female **chicken** is called a hen.*

Circle *noun*
A closed ring or solid shape that has no corners and is exactly round.

*The gong is shaped like a **circle**.*

Clam *noun*
A water animal that has a soft body inside two hinged shells.

Clams need their shells to protect their soft bodies.

Clarinet *noun*
A long, narrow musical instrument played by blowing into one end while pressing down on its keys.

*You can often hear the **clarinet** being played in classical and jazz music.*

Climb *verb*
To move toward the top of something.

*SpongeBob and Patrick **climb** the ropes.*

Clock *noun*
A machine that shows the time.

*This is a funny-looking **clock**.*

Clean *adjective*
Free of dirt or messiness. *Clean* is the opposite of *dirty*.

*Dog makes a mess, while Cat keeps things **clean**.*

Close *adverb*
Nearby.

*Phil and Lil are sitting **close** to each other.*

Clothes *noun*
The things we wear to cover our bodies.

*The **clothes** Ginger is wearing are a yellow shirt and blue pants.*

Cockatoo *noun*
A white bird that is a type of parrot.

*Some people keep a **cockatoo** as a pet and train it to talk.*

Cold *adjective*
Not warm or hot. *Cold* is the opposite of *hot.*

*When it's **cold** out, Eliza stays warm in her winter coat.*

Color *noun*
The light reflected or absorbed by objects that makes them all look different.

*A painter uses different **colors.***

ORANGE
LIGHT BLUE
BLACK
YELLOW
WHITE
BLUE
RED

Coffee *noun*
A drink made from coffee beans.

*Many people drink **coffee** in the morning.*

Come *verb*
To get to one place from another.

*Would you like to **come** to CatDog's party?*

Comfortable *adjective*

Nice to touch, wear, or be in or around.

CatDog love their couch because it is so **comfortable**.

Cone *noun*

A shape that is round at one end and pointy at the other.

The scoop of ice cream is on the **cone**.

Community *noun*

A town or neighborhood where people live.

A.J. and Chester live in the same **community**.

Confident *adjective*

Sure that you can do something.

Jenny is **confident** that she can fight evil.

ASIA NORTH AMERICA EUROPE AFRICA AUSTRALIA SOUTH AMERICA ANTARCTICA

Computer *noun*

A machine people use at work and at home to create, store, and find information.

Jimmy uses his **computer** to help him remember his inventions.

Continent *noun*

A large body of land separated from others by water or another division.

There are seven **continents** on Earth.

Cooler noun
A container that keeps food and drinks cold.

*Drinks will stay cool at the beach if you keep them in a **cooler**.*

Cornucopia noun
A horn-shaped basket filled with fruits, vegetables, and grains.

*A **cornucopia** is often used as a decoration at Thanksgiving.*

Corn noun
A vegetable with many small kernels, or seeds, attached to a long cob, or stalk.

Corn can be eaten on or off the cob.

Costume noun
An outfit you dress up in to look like someone else.

*Timmy's **costume** includes a cape and a mask.*

Couch noun
A seat big enough for two or more people.

*Can you guess which side of the **couch** Dog sits on?*

Corner noun
The point where two lines meet.

*Arnold and Gerald are standing on the street **corner**.*

Count verb
To say numbers in order to reach an amount or to know how many objects there are.

*Darwin **counts** on each of his toes.*

37

Cow *noun*
An animal raised on a farm or ranch for its milk or for beef.

The cow is black and white.

Crab *noun*
An animal with a hard shell and pointy claws.

Mr. Krabs is not your ordinary crab.

Crown *noun*
A special headpiece worn by kings, queens, or fairy godparents.

Cosmo and Wanda each wear a gold crown.

Crawl *verb*
To move on your hands and knees.

Kimi crawls when adults are nearby.

Cry *verb*
To have tears coming from your eyes because you feel sad or upset.

Dil starts to cry because the crab has his pacifier.

Crocodile *noun*
A water animal with a long, strong jaw full of sharp teeth and a long, low body covered with thick, bumpy skin.

It is easy to confuse a crocodile with an alligator but its head is more pointed and its sharp teeth stick out when its mouth is closed.

Cup *noun*
A container used for drinking.

Presto! Like magic, Cosmo turns into a cup.

Curious *adjective*
Wanting to learn or find out about new things.

*Eliza is not the only one who is **curious** about gorillas!*

GORILLA
IN THE
MIDST

Dance *verb*
To move your body to music.

*Carl likes to **dance** the jitterbug. If only he didn't step on his own two feet!*

Dd

Dad *noun*
A male parent.

*Timmy's **dad** is very proud of his son.*

Darts *noun*
A game in which you throw pointed objects at a target to score points.

*In **darts**, the center of the dartboard is called the bull's eye.*

Daisy *noun*
A flower with petals and a yellow center.

*Helga picks the petals off the **daisy**. "He loves me . . . he loves me not . . ."*

Daydream *verb*
To become lost in your own thoughts.

*Jenny **daydreams** about the school dance.*

Decide *verb*
To make up your mind about something.

*Gerald tries to **decide** what to do next.*

Delicious *adjective*
Tasty.

*The apple looks **delicious.***

Deep *adjective*
Having lots of room between the top and the bottom.

*CatDog's pool is not **deep.***

Deliver *verb*
To bring something from one place to another.

*Carts are used to **deliver** luggage to the airplane.*

Defend *verb*
To protect something or someone from harm.

*Jenny works hard to **defend** her friends from evil.*

Dentist *noun*
A person trained to care for teeth and gums.

*Brush your teeth every day and visit the **dentist** twice a year.*

Describe verb
To tell about something.

*Angelica uses her arms to **describe** how big a star she is!*

Different adjective
Not the same. *Different* is the opposite of *alike*.

*These two animals are both dogs, but they look **different**.*

Dessert noun
A food often eaten at the end of a meal.

*Those cupcakes aren't **dessert**! They're Wanda and Cosmo.*

Difficult adjective
Hard to do. *Difficult* is the opposite of *easy*.

*SpongeBob does a **difficult** skateboard trick.*

Dig verb
To scoop something up.

*Dil uses his shovel to **dig** a hole in the snow.*

Dictionary noun
A book that lists words and their meanings.

*You can use a **dictionary** to learn new words.*

DICTIONARY

41

Dinner noun
A meal eaten at the end of the day.

*Chicken, spaghetti, and tacos are popular foods for **dinner**.*

Dirty adjective
Messy or not clean.
***Dirty** is the opposite of **clean**.*

*Cosmo should clean his **dirty** socks.*

Dinosaur noun
A large animal that used to live on Earth a long time ago.

*Tommy is dressed like a **dinosaur** for Halloween.*

DISAPPEAR!

Disappear verb
To go out of sight.
***Disappear** is the opposite of **appear**.*

*Wanda uses her magic to make things **disappear**.*

Diploma noun
An official paper given to you when you have successfully completed a school.

*Many people will hang their **diploma** on the wall.*

Disappointed adjective
How you feel when something you expected or hoped for does not happen.

*Patrick is **disappointed** that his Krabby Patty fell.*

Disguise *verb*
To hide what something looks like by making it look different.

*SpongeBob is **disguised** as a ghost.*

Dog *noun*
A furry pet animal that barks and wags its tail.

*A **dog** is sometimes called man's best friend.*

Dive *verb*
To jump into something headfirst.

*Wanda likes to **dive** into the pool.*

Doll *noun*
A toy that looks like a small person.

*Angelica's favorite **doll** is Cynthia.*

Do *verb*
To make something happen.

*When Cosmo and Wanda **do** their magic, crazy things happen.*

Doctor *noun*
A person trained to help you when you are sick or injured.

*SpongeBob is dressed up as a **doctor**.*

Dolphin *noun*
A large water animal with a large nose.

*The **dolphin** is known to be smart and friendly.*

43

DOORKNOB

Door *noun*
An entrance to a house, building, or car.

Draw *verb*
To make a picture with a pencil, pen, or crayon.

*You use chalk to **draw** on a chalkboard.*

Doorknob *noun*
A handle for a door.

*To open the **door**, you need to turn the **doorknob** and push or pull.*

Dress *verb*
To put clothes on.

*When you go skiing, be sure to **dress** in warm clothing.*

Double *adjective*
Twice as much or twice as big.

*There's **double** trouble when Phil and Lil are around.*

Drink *verb*
To put a liquid in your mouth and swallow it.

*Patrick **drinks** from a plastic cup.*

Dragonfly *noun*
An insect with a long, thin body and big wings.

*Donnie chases the **dragonfly**.*

Drop *verb*
To let something fall by letting go of it.

*Arnold got scared and **dropped** his flashlight.*

44

Drum *noun*
A circular musical instrument played by hitting it with sticks or your hands.

Squidward plays his drum.

Eagle *noun*
A bird with a curved beak and large wings.

The bald eagle is the national bird of the United States.

Ee

Earmuffs *noun*
Two pads, connected by a headband, that you wear to keep your ears warm.

Angelica is wearing earmuffs.

Dry *adjective*
Not wet.

Donnie is dry but Debbie is very, very wet!

Easy *adjective*
Not hard to do. *Easy* is the opposite of *difficult*.

It's easy to have a good time playing soccer.

Duck *noun*
A bird with a flat bill and webbed feet that quacks.

A duck swims with most of its body above the water.

Eat *verb*
To chew and swallow food.

*Dog likes to **eat** dog food but Cat does not!*

Electricity *noun*
Power that makes machines work and lights turn on.

*The street lamp lights up with **electricity**.*

Egg *noun*
A round object, laid by a female animal, that holds an unborn baby animal. A baby animal is born when the egg hatches.

*This is a chicken **egg**.*

Elephant *noun*
A large animal with floppy ears and a long trunk.

*Eliza and Darwin are riding an **elephant**.*

8

Eight *adjective*
A number greater than seven and less than nine.

*There are **eight** bells.*

Election *noun*
The time when people vote to choose a leader.

*In the United States, an **election** is held every four years to pick a president.*

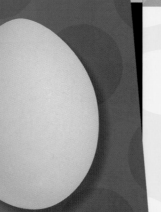

Eleven *adjective*
A number greater than ten and less than twelve.

*There are **eleven** footballs.*

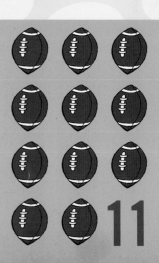

11

E-mail *noun*
A letter you send by computer.

*SpongeBob uses his computer to send an **e-mail** to Patrick.*

Enjoy *verb*
To really like doing something.

*Dil and Tommy **enjoy** playing together.*

Emotion *noun*
A feeling such as happiness, sadness, anger, or excitement.

*Patrick is showing the **emotion** called happiness!*

Envelope *noun*
A covering for a letter.

*There are many **envelopes** in the mailbox.*

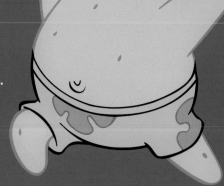

End *verb*
To come to the last part of something. *End* is the opposite of *start* or *begin*.

*Angelica is about to **end** her song.*

Equal *adjective*
The same in size or amount.

*The number of eggs is **equal** to the number of cookies.*

47

Equator *noun*
An imaginary line around the middle of the Earth.

The line on the globe shows where the equator is located.

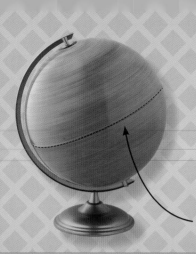

EQUATOR

Exercise *verb*
To do an activity over and over to make your body healthy and strong.

Patrick exercises by touching his toes.

Equipment *noun*
Supplies you use to do something.

This equipment could be used for playing during recess at school.

Exit *noun*
A way out of a building or other space.

Usually, an exit is marked with a sign.

EXIT

Even *adjective*
Able to be divided in half with nothing left over. *Even* is the opposite of *odd*.

There is an even number of blocks— two!

Excited *adjective*
Really happy.

SpongeBob is excited about his birthday party.

Expect *verb*
To believe that something will happen.

Does Plankton expect to be able to steal the Krabby Patty recipe? Yes, he does!

Explore *verb*
To search, see, learn, and do new things.

*Eliza **explores** the sea with her new friend.*

Fact *noun*
A true piece of information.

*It is a **fact** that Eliza loves animals!*

Extreme *adjective*
Beyond what is normal.

*SpongeBob and Patrick's sadness was **extreme** when the amusement park was closed.*

Fair *adverb*
Treating everyone the same way.

*Gerald plays **fair** by waiting his turn.*

Eyeglasses *noun*
Objects with glass or plastic lenses worn in front of the eyes to help people see better.

*Eliza wears **eyeglasses**.*

Fairy tale *noun*
A story about magic, often including fairies or other make-believe creatures.

*Angelica looks like she stepped out of a **fairy tale**.*

Fall *verb*
To drop toward the ground.

Debbie and Donnie **fall** *through the air.*

Fan *noun*
A machine that blows air to help keep people or things cool.

Jimmy cools down his hot drink with a **fan** *attached to his mug.*

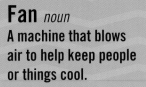

Family *noun*
A group of people related to each other.

The Neutrons are a **family**.

Far *adverb*
Not close by. *Far* is the opposite of *near*.

SpongeBob's hands are **far** *apart.*

Famous *adjective*
Known by many people.

Angelica dreams of being **famous** *one day.*

Fast *adjective*
Moving quickly. *Fast* is the opposite of *slow*.

Even with her big boots, Sandy Cheeks is a very **fast** *runner.*

Fat *adjective*
Very large and plump.

*The pig has a **fat** belly.*

Feed *verb*
To give food to.

*Eliza **feeds** flowers to the zebra.*

Feel *verb*
To touch something.

*Gross! SpongeBob **feels** his brain.*

Favorite *adjective*
Liked more than anything else.

*Patrick's **favorite** thing to do is play with his best buddy, SpongeBob.*

Feather *noun*
The hairlike covering on birds that helps them stay warm and fly smoothly.

*Parrots have brightly colored **feathers**.*

Fill *verb*
To put as much into something as it can hold.

*Angelica **fills** Susie's hood with snow.*

51

Find verb
To discover or locate something.

*Eliza **finds** sleeping lion cubs in the bushes.*

Fire truck noun
A truck that carries firefighters and their equipment.

*A **fire truck** is often painted red so that it is easy for people in other vehicles to see it.*

First adjective
Coming before all others. *First* is the opposite of *last*.

*When you come in **first** place in a race or contest, you often get a blue ribbon.*

1st PLACE

Fire noun
The flame made when something burns.

*The **fire** burns on the logs.*

Firefighter noun
A person trained to put out fires.

*While on the job, a **firefighter** wears a special protective helmet like this one.*

Fish noun
A water animal with fins to help it swim and gills so it can breathe in water.

*Cosmo and Wanda make very funny-looking **fish**!*

Fishing *noun*
Trying to catch fish.

When SpongeBob and Patrick go **fishing,** they catch a Krabby Patty!

Flag *noun*
A piece of cloth with a special design on it that stands for a country, state, or other group.

The **flag** of the United States is red, white, and blue.

Flap *verb*
To wave up and down.

When a duck flies, it has to **flap** its wings.

Five *adjective*
A number greater than four and less than six.

There are **five** stars.

5

Fizzy *adjective*
Filled with bubbles.

Patrick's **fizzy** drink tickles his nose.

Flashlight *noun*
A small object you can carry that uses batteries to produce light.

Danny uses a **flashlight** to see in the dark.

Flavor noun
How something tastes.

*The **flavor** of this ice cream is vanilla.*

Flute noun
A musical instrument that is a long, thin metal tube with a mouthpiece and keys.

*A **flute** is played by blowing air over its opening while pressing on the keys.*

Flip-flops noun
Shoes held on to your feet by a strip that fits between your toes.

*SpongeBob wears **flip-flops** at the beach.*

Flutter verb
To move up and down quickly.

*Butterflies **flutter** their wings to move.*

Flippers noun
Shoes worn for swimming that look like webbed feet.

***Flippers** help you move through water.*

Flower noun
The colorful part of a plant or tree that blossoms and makes fruit or seeds.

*Cosmo has **flowers** for Wanda.*

Fly verb
To move through the air without touching the ground.

*Danny Phantom can **fly** almost as fast as an airplane.*

Food *noun*
What people and animals eat to get energy to live and grow.

Bread, carrots, and pizza are all types of food.

Football *noun*
A game played by two teams on a large field where they take turns trying to get an oval ball to a goal.

Arnold and Gerald enjoy playing football.

Forgive *verb*
To stop being angry about something someone did or said.

After Wanda decides to forgive Cosmo for making a mess of things, she gives him a hug.

Fork *noun*
A tool with prongs used to pick up food for eating.

You use a fork to eat pancakes.

Footprint *noun*
A mark made by a foot or shoe.

Whose footprint is that?

Four *adjective*
A number greater than three and less than five.

There are four sandwiches.

4

Fox *noun*
A small, furry animal with a thick, bushy tail and a pointy nose.

*The **fox** is known for being smart and hard to catch.*

Friend *noun*
A person you like to spend time with.

*Timmy is Chester's **friend**.*

Frog *noun*
A small, green animal with strong back legs used for hopping.

*Donnie catches flies with his friend, the **frog**.*

Freckles *noun*
Small, brownish spots on the skin.

*Chuckie has **freckles** on his cheeks.*

Freeze *verb*
To become very cold and hard.

*When you **freeze** juice, you get a tasty treat!*

Front *noun*
The first part, or the part of something that faces forward.

*Angelica is at the **front** of the line.*

Frown *verb*
To make an unhappy face when you are sad or displeased.

*Darwin **frowns** to show he doesn't like being cold.*

Funny *adjective*
Making people smile or laugh.

*SpongeBob is making a **funny** face.*

Fruit *noun*
The part of a plant that has seeds and is often used as food.

*Eating **fruit** is part of a healthy diet.*

Full *adjective*
Holding all that can be held.

*Patrick's mouth is **full** of snowballs.*

Fur *noun*
The soft hair that grows on some animals.

*The dog's **fur** keeps her warm.*

Fun *adjective*
Pleasant and enjoyable.

*For SpongeBob, even mopping is **fun**!*

Furniture *noun*
Movable objects in a building, such as tables, chairs, couches, and beds.

*A chair is a piece of **furniture** you can sit on.*

Gg

Garden noun
An area for growing flowers and plants.

Susie plants flowers in her garden.

Garlic noun
An herb that grows in the ground as a bulb and is used to flavor food.

Garlic has a very strong smell.

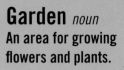

Galaxy noun
A large group of stars.

Jimmy flies his rocket through the galaxy to learn about planets and stars.

Game noun
An activity you do for fun.

Pin the Tail on the Donkey is a game.

Ghost noun
A make-believe spirit.

This ghost looks very scary.

Garbage truck noun
A truck that garbage is loaded into so it can be taken away.

The garbage truck is on its way to the dump.

Giant adjective
Very big.

Jorgen has a giant wand.

Gift *noun*
A present you give to someone.

*Chuckie is opening his **gift.***

Glass *noun*
A hard, smooth material used to make containers, windows, and decorations.

*The milk bottle is made of **glass**.*

Giraffe *noun*
A tall animal with a long neck and a sticky tongue.

*A **giraffe** uses its tongue to grab leaves from very tall trees.*

Glitter *noun*
A sparkly material used for decorations and art projects.

*This ornament has **glitter** on it.*

Globe *noun*
A model of the world.

*Cat finds countries on his **globe**.*

Girl *noun*
A child who is not a boy.

*Susie is a **girl**, and so is Kimi.*

Gloves *noun*

Coverings for your hands with a separate pocket for each finger and your thumb.

*When working in the garden, it's a good idea to wear **gloves**.*

Goat *noun*

A farm animal that eats grass and many other plants and has rough hair.

*A baby **goat** is called a kid.*

Goggles *noun*

Safety glasses that protect your eyes when you work or play.

*Maddie Fenton always wears **goggles** when she goes ghost hunting.*

Go *verb*

To move from one place to another.

*You can **go** fast on a bicycle and a skateboard.*

Gold *noun*

A shiny, yellow metal often used to make jewelry or coins.

*Debbie discovers a chest of **gold**.*

Goal *noun*

The part of a playing area where you can score points when you move a ball or other object into it.

*Sam tries to make a **goal**.*

Goldfish noun
A small yellow or orange fish.

Goldfish are good animals to keep as pets.

Golf noun
A game played on a grassy course with a ball and clubs.

*To play **golf**, SpongeBob uses a golf club to hit the ball into a hole.*

Grab verb
To reach for something and hold on.

*Reggie must **grab** her snowboard to do this trick in the air.*

Good adjective
Pleasant or useful; not bad.

*SpongeBob gets lots of stars at boating school because he has been so **good**.*

GOOD NOODLES

SpongeBob	★★★★★★★★★★
Lloyd	★
Sheila	★
Paco	★★
Debbie	★★★
Horace	★

Grapes noun
Small, round fruit that grow in bunches and can be red, green, or black.

*If **grapes** are left out to dry for a long time, they will turn into raisins.*

Gorilla noun
A large, strong ape with a stocky body and thick, dark hair.

*Chuckie is pretending to be a **gorilla**.*

Grapefruit noun
A large, round citrus fruit that can be yellow or pink.

*A **grapefruit** has a slightly sour taste.*

Grass *noun*
Tiny plants grown to cover large areas of ground.

*Patrick stands in the tall **grass**.*

Gross *adjective*
Really yucky or disgusting.

*An eyeball in a jar is pretty **gross**.*

Great *adjective*
Really good.

*CatDog are having a **great** time at the party.*

Grow *verb*
To become larger.

*One day, these puppies will **grow** up to be big dogs.*

Guinea pig *noun*
A small, furry animal that people keep as pets.

*The **guinea pig** likes to eat seeds and nuts.*

Green bean *noun*
A thin, green vegetable that grows on a tall plant.

***Green beans** are healthy.*

Guitar *noun*
A musical instrument played by strumming your fingers across its strings.

*For a very loud sound, some people play an electric **guitar**.*

Hair dryer *noun*
A machine that blows hot air on your hair to dry it quickly.

*Debbie's **hair dryer** is very powerful!*

Hamster *noun*
A small animal with short fur that people keep as a pet.

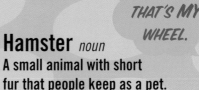

HEY! THAT'S MY WHEEL.

*This **hamster** wants to exercise, but Sandy Cheeks is jogging on its wheel!*

Half *noun*
One of two evenly divided parts.

*Each **half** of the kiwi is the same size.*

Hammer *noun*
A tool with a handle and a heavy metal head used for striking or pounding.

*You must be careful when using a **hammer**.*

Handle *noun*
The part of an object, like a cup, that you hold on to.

*Wanda's **handle** is pink.*

Hammock *noun*
A hanging chair.

*A **hammock** is a nice place to take a nap.*

Handstand *noun*
A pose in which you stand on your hands with your feet up in the air.

*Twister does a one-handed **handstand**.*

63

Hang *verb*
To be attached to something above.

*Eliza and Darwin **hang** from a tree branch.*

Hare *noun*
An animal related to the rabbit, but larger and with longer ears.

*The **hare** lives wild in the countryside, where it runs very fast.*

Harmonica *noun*
A small musical instrument played by blowing across a row of air holes.

*Arnold plays a song on his **harmonica**.*

Happy *adjective*
Feeling good and cheerful. *Happy* is the opposite of *sad*.

*Cosmo and Wanda are always **happy** to help Timmy.*

Harp *noun*
A large musical instrument played by plucking its strings.

*The frame of a **harp** is usually shaped like a triangle.*

Hard *adjective*
Firm. *Hard* is the opposite of *soft*.

*Wearing a **hard** hat will protect your head from falling objects.*

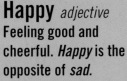

Hat *noun*
A covering for your head.

*Susie wears a party **hat**.*

Headache *noun*
A pain in your head.

*When SpongeBob and Patrick are too loud, Squidward gets a **headache**.*

Heart *noun*
A shape that has the same name as the organ that pumps blood through our bodies.

*A **heart** makes us think of love.*

Headstand *noun*
A pose in which you stand on your head, supported by your hands, with your feet up in the air.

*Hoodsey can do a **headstand**.*

Heat *verb*
To make something warm.

*A stove is used to **heat** food.*

Healthy *adjective*
Well and strong, without disease or illness.

*To be a superhero, you have to be strong and **healthy**.*

Hear *verb*
To use your ears to listen to sounds.

*SpongeBob thinks he can **hear** the sea through the seashell.*

Heavy *adjective*
Not easy to lift, because of weight. *Heavy* is the opposite of *light*.

*Jorgen lifts a **heavy** weight.*

65

Helicopter *noun*
An aircraft with rotating blades.

*The propeller of the **helicopter** goes around and around.*

Hero *noun*
A person admired for his or her strength and courage.

*The Crimson Chin is Cleft's **hero**.*

Helmet *noun*
A hard hat worn to protect your head.

*SpongeBob wears a **helmet** when he rides his dirt bike.*

Hide *verb*
To put something where no one can see it.

*Chuckie **hides** a gift behind his back.*

Help *verb*
To make it easier for someone to do something.

*Kimi **helps** Chuckie take off his shoes.*

High *adjective*
Far from the ground.
***High** is the opposite of low.*

*SpongeBob does a **high** kick.*

Hippopotamus *noun*
A large animal with short legs and a big mouth.

*The **hippopotamus** looks big and clumsy but is very graceful in the water.*

Hole *noun*
An opening or tear in something.

*Oops! SpongeBob has a **hole** in his pants.*

Hit *verb*
To touch something with force.

*You **hit** a baseball with a baseball bat.*

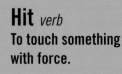

Holiday *noun*
A special day when people honor something that happened in the past.

*The Fourth of July is a **holiday** for people to celebrate America's birthday.*

Hockey *noun*
A game played by two teams using curved sticks to try to drive a puck into a goal.

*Otto loves a good game of **hockey**.*

Hoop *noun*
A circular strip of wood, plastic, or rubber.

*Susie twirls two **hoops** around her waist.*

Hop *verb*
To jump up and down.

*Helga **hops** from square to square.*

Horse *noun*
A large animal with strong legs, a mane, and a long tail.

*A **horse** can run long distances.*

Hot *adjective*
Very warm. *Hot* is the opposite of *cold*.

*Tommy's drink is **hot**.*

Horseshoe *noun*
A flat metal plate fixed onto a horse's hoof to protect it.

*A blacksmith fits a **horseshoe** to each hoof, molding the metal to its exact shape.*

Hot dog *noun*
Chopped-up meat shaped into tubes.

***Hot dogs** are a popular food at baseball games.*

Hose *noun*
A hollow rubber tube used to carry water.

*A **hose** can be used to wash cars, clean an outdoor deck, or water plants.*

Hour *noun*
A period of sixty minutes.

*It is now three o'clock. In one **hour**, it will be four o'clock.*

House *noun*
A building where people live.

*The **house** has three floors.*

Hurt *verb*
To cause or to be in pain.

*Get out a big roll of bandages—Patrick **hurt** himself.*

Hug *verb*
To put your arms around someone or something.

*Darwin **hugs** the tree branch so he doesn't fall.*

Husband *noun*
A man who is married.

*Hugh Neutron is Judy Neutron's **husband**.*

Hungry *adjective*
Feeling the need to eat.

*The **hungry** dog eats his food.*

Hyena *noun*
A furry animal that looks like a dog.

*The **hyena** is known for a noise it makes that sounds like laughing.*

I i

Ice noun
Frozen water.

Put cubes of ice in a drink to keep it cold.

Identify verb
To call something by name.

Can you identify who's upside-down? Bet you can!

Ice cream noun
A frozen dessert made from cream, eggs, and sugar.

The ice cream is melting down the sides of the cone.

Igloo noun
A house made of ice or packed snow.

Timmy makes a tiny igloo.

Icicle noun
A spike of ice made when dripping water freezes in midair.

Brrr! Icicles form on Cosmo and Wanda's bowl.

Idea noun
A thought or plan.

Making faces at the fish is a funny idea.

Iguana noun
A large lizard with spikes running along its back.

You might not want to keep an iguana as a pet because these lizards grow to be very large!

Imagine *verb*
To make a picture of something in your mind.

*Helga **imagines** a great love story starring Arnold to write in her notebook, even though it is just make-believe!*

Impossible *adjective*
Not able to be done.

*Grandpa knows that if you set your mind to something, nothing is **impossible**.*

Immediately *adverb*
Right away.

*Squidward wants to get away from this jellyfish **immediately!***

In *preposition*
Within or inside something. *In* is the opposite of *out*.

*SpongeBob and Patrick are **in** the box.*

Important *adjective*
Meaning a lot or having a lot of power.

*Mr. Krabs thinks making lots and lots of money is **important**.*

Inch *noun*
A small measurement used to show an object's length, height, or distance.

*This measuring tape helps you measure an object in **inches**.*

Information *noun*
Facts about something.

*SpongeBob uses the walkie-talkie to give Patrick **information**.*

Injure *verb*
To hurt a part of your body.

*This snowball didn't **injure** Squidward, it just surprised him.*

Internet *noun*
A system that connects computers all around the world.

*Using the **Internet**, SpongeBob can send pictures to his friends, no matter where they live.*

Insect *noun*
A small animal with six legs and a body separated into three parts.

*An **insect** usually has wings.*

Invention *noun*
Something that has never been made before.

*Jimmy Neutron's **invention** blocks others from tackling him.*

Inside *preposition*
Within or on the inner side of something. *Inside* is the opposite of *outside*.

*The letter is **inside** the bottle.*

Dear Santa

Invisible *adjective*
Unable to be seen.

*Chuckie is afraid of an **invisible** bogeyman.*

Island _noun_
An area of land surrounded by water.

Wanda and Cosmo enjoy the view from the **island**.

Jacket _noun_
A short coat.

SpongeBob looks hip in his leather **jacket**.

Jack-o'-lantern _noun_
A pumpkin that is carved to look like a face and lit with a candle placed inside.

People put **jack-o'-lanterns** in their windows for Halloween.

Itch _noun_
An irritating feeling on your skin that makes you want to scratch.

Tommy has an **itch** on his head.

Jacks _noun_
A game played with a small ball and several six-pointed metal or plastic pieces.

You can play **jacks** alone or with a friend.

Ivy _noun_
A leafy green plant that can grow up walls or trees.

**Ivy** is sometimes called a climbing plant because it often grows up the sides of houses and walls.

Jaguar _noun_
A large, spotted wild cat that lives in the jungle.

A **jaguar** can run almost as fast as its cousin, the cheetah.

Jeans *noun*
Pants made out of a strong cloth called denim.

*Timmy looks sharp in his sunglasses and **jeans**.*

Job *noun*
A task or work that must be done.

*Captain Plankton's **job** is to sail the boat.*

Jellyfish *noun*
A sea animal with a soft body and long tentacles.

*Ouch! SpongeBob got stung by a **jellyfish**.*

Joke *noun*
A riddle or story with a funny ending.

*Patrick and SpongeBob are laughing about a funny **joke**.*

Jigsaw puzzle *noun*
A picture cut up into shaped pieces that can be put back together for fun.

*Putting together a **jigsaw puzzle** is great to do on a rainy day.*

Juggle *verb*
To keep two or more things in the air at the same time by tossing them quickly again and again.

*Kimi likes to **juggle** cookies.*

Juice *noun*
A drink made from fruit.

Orange juice is good for you.

Kangaroo *noun*
An animal that can jump far and carry its young in its pouch.

A kangaroo hops to get from place to place.

Kk

Jump *verb*
To move into the air so your feet leave the ground.

Danny Phantom can jump high.

Jump rope *noun*
A rope you twirl and jump over for fun or exercise.

You can play with a jump rope alone or with a friend.

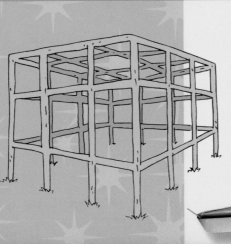

Karate *noun*
A sport in which opponents use special kicking and hand movements.

SpongeBob works on his karate kick with Sandy Cheeks.

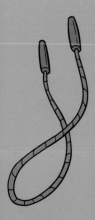

Jungle gym *noun*
A set of poles, bars, and slides connected together to climb and play on.

During recess, kids play on the jungle gym.

Kayak *noun*
A small, narrow boat for one or two people who each use a paddle with a blade on each end to move through water.

Eskimos used to make kayaks from animal skins and a wooden frame so they could fish in the icy ocean.

Kk

Keep *verb*
To hold on to as your own.

*Courtney likes to **keep** a mirror in her pocket to make sure her hair looks nice.*

Kick *verb*
To strike something with your foot.

*Arnold **kicks** the football high.*

Ketchup *noun*
A sauce made from tomatoes.

*French fries taste good with **ketchup**.*

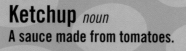

Kid *noun*
A child.

*Tommy is not a baby anymore. He is a 10-year-old **kid** now!*

Kettle *noun*
A pot used to boil water.

*Wanda has turned herself into a **kettle**.*

Key *noun*
A small, shaped piece of metal turned to open or close a lock.

*A **key** unlocks the front door.*

Kind *adjective*
Friendly and nice.

*Arnold is **kind** to everyone. Well, everyone but Helga.*

Kiss *verb*
To touch someone with your lips.

*Kimi **kisses** Chuckie.*

Knife *noun*
A tool with a blade used for cutting.

*Ask an adult before you use a **knife**.*

Kiwi *noun*
An oval-shaped fruit that is green with tiny black seeds on the inside and covered with a fuzzy brown skin on the outside.

*Have you ever eaten a **kiwi**?*

Kitten *noun*
A young cat.

*A **kitten** is a very playful animal that loves to chase and pounce on toys.*

Knock *verb*
To strike something with a hard blow.

*Reggie uses her hockey stick to **knock** the puck into the goal.*

Kneel *noun*
To rest on one or both knees.

*Angelica **kneels** as she sings her song.*

Ladybug *noun*
A small, rounded beetle that is often red or orange with black dots.

How many dots are on the ladybug?

Knot *noun*
A section of a rope, cord, or ribbon laced together, forming a bump.

CatDog have tied themselves into a knot.

Lamb *noun*
A young sheep.

A lamb has soft wool used for making sweaters, blankets, and socks.

Koala *noun*
A furry animal with big ears and a black nose.

Koala bears are related to kangaroos, not bears!

Lamp *noun*
An object that gives off light.

Helga looks lovingly at Arnold from behind the street lamp.

L l

Ladder *noun*
A frame with two long sides crossed with rungs or steps for climbing up and down.

Tommy climbs up the ladder to put the star on top of the tree.

Language *noun*
All the words you use when you speak or write.

*In addition to English and Russian, Plankton's uncle speaks the **language** called Planktonese.*

Large *adjective*
Big.

*Compared to the cat, the dog looks **large**.*

Later *adverb*
After right now. *Later* is the opposite of *now*.

*The Rugrats are dancing now; **later** they will have cake.*

Last *adjective*
Coming after all others. *Last* is the opposite of *first*.

*Arnold does not want to come in **last** place in the arm-wrestling contest.*

Laugh *verb*
To smile and make sounds to show something is funny.

*If you **laugh** at other people's report cards, you will not win friends.*

Late *adjective*
Happening after the expected or correct time.

*Squidward hates to wait, so don't be **late**.*

Lawn mower *noun*
A machine used to cut grass.

*Jimmy Neutron saves time with his super-powerful **lawn mower**.*

Lawyer *noun*
A person trained to know about laws and give advice about them to others.

Lawyers often wear suits and carry briefcases.

Left *adjective*
The side or direction opposite the right. *Left* is the opposite of *right*.

*The arrow is pointing to the **left** side of this page.*

Leaf *noun*
The thin, green, flat part of a plant attached to it by a stem.

*Eliza and her friends take a ride in a **leaf**.*

Lemonade *noun*
A drink made with lemons, water, and sugar.

*When it's hot outside, drinking **lemonade** can cool you down.*

Lettuce *noun*
A leafy green vegetable.

Lettuce is often eaten in sandwiches and salads.

Learn *verb*
To find out new things.

*You can **learn** a lot by reading books.*

Life jacket *noun*
A vest made of a special material that helps you float in water.

*Wear a **life jacket** when you go on a boat.*

Light *adjective*
Easy to lift. *Light* is the opposite of *heavy*.

Feather pillows are **light** and fluffy, perfect for pillow fights!

Lightning *noun*
A quick flash of electricity in the sky during a thunderstorm.

Usually, when there's **lightning**, you're sure to hear thunder.

Light *adjective*
Not dark.

A flashlight or lamp can make a dark room **light**.

Like *verb*
To enjoy something or someone.

Helga **likes** Arnold a lot.

Lightbulb *noun*
The part of a lamp that gives off light.

A **lightbulb** lights up when you turn on a lamp.

Lime *noun*
A small, green citrus fruit.

Lime is used as a flavoring for desserts and drinks.

Lion *noun*
A large wild cat that lives in a group called a pride.

*A male **lion** has a mane that goes all around his head.*

Lock *noun*
An object used to keep things closed and secure.

*This **lock** can be opened using a key.*

Little *adjective*
Small. ***Little*** is the opposite of *big*.

*Jimmy Neutron was a cute **little** baby!*

Log *noun*
A piece of a tree trunk that has been cut or has fallen away.

*These **log**s have been cut to use as firewood.*

Lizard *noun*
A four-legged reptile with a long body covered in scales.

*This **lizard** has a frilled neck to scare other animals away.*

Long *adjective*
Having a large amount of time or space from beginning to end. ***Long*** is the opposite of *short*.

*What a **long** neck Goddard has when he stretches it out!*

Lobster *noun*
A sea animal with a body covered in a hard shell and ten legs, including two with big pinching claws.

*Some people enjoy eating **lobster** for dinner.*

Look *verb*
To use your eyes to see something.

Look into the camera and smile, Nigel!

Lost *adjective*
Missing or unable to be found.

Danny's favorite comic book is **lost**.

Low *adjective*
Close to the ground. *Low* is the opposite of *high*.

SpongeBob finds an egg in the **low** grass.

Lucky *adjective*
Having good things happen to you by chance. *Lucky* is the opposite of *unlucky*.

Some people think that it is **lucky** to find a four leafed clover. Keep looking Patrick!

Loud *adjective*
Noisy. *Loud* is the opposite of *quiet*.

When SpongeBob plays his guitar, he is always very **loud**!

Lunch *noun*
A meal eaten in the middle of the day.

What is your favorite thing to eat for **lunch**?

Love *verb*
To care for someone or something.

Cosmo and Wanda **love** each other very much.

Machine *noun*
An object used to help people do work or make things.

*This **machine** makes copies of papers.*

Magician *noun*
A person who does tricks that seem like magic.

*Just like a **magician**, Tommy knows lots of card tricks.*

Mm

Magnet *noun*
A piece of metal that can pull other metal items toward itself.

*This **magnet** has a powerful force.*

Mad *adjective*
Very angry.

*When Mrs. Neutron folds her arms, you know she is **mad** about something.*

Magnifying glass *noun*
A lens that makes objects look bigger.

*Plankton is still tiny, even when seen through a **magnifying glass**!*

Magazine *noun*
Pages of words and pictures joined together like a book and published regularly.

*Debbie is reading her favorite **magazine**.*

Mail *noun*
Letters and packages delivered by a postal service.

*When **mail** is delivered to your house, it is placed in your mailbox.*

Mammal *noun*
A warm-blooded animal that is born live and feeds on its mother's milk when first born.

*Dolphins and elephants are very different animals, but they are each a type of **mammal**.*

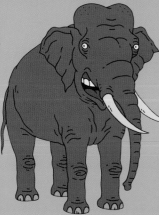

Maraca *noun*
A musical instrument containing beads or beans that makes noise when shaken.

*Musicians usually hold one **maraca** in each hand.*

Marble *noun*
A small glass ball used for playing games.

*Pick your favorite **marble**.*

Man *noun*
A grown-up boy.

*Nigel Thornberry is such a brave **man**, he's not even scared of this snake.*

March *verb*
To walk along to a set rhythm.

*In a parade, bands **march** and play music.*

Map *noun*
A drawing that shows where places are located.

*Eliza checks her **map** to make sure she doesn't get lost.*

Mask *noun*
A covering for your face.

*The feathers on this **mask** make it look festive.*

Match *verb*
To look the same or have the same features.

*Two of these shapes **match**.*

Microscope *noun*
A tool used to take a close look at small things.

*The powerful lens of the **microscope** makes things appear much larger.*

Measure *verb*
To find out something's size, weight, or volume.

*This tape can be pulled out farther to **measure** very long things.*

Milk *noun*
The white liquid produced by cows and other mammals to feed their young.

*Lots of babies drink **milk**.*

Medal *noun*
A flat piece of metal, often with a ribbon attached, awarded to someone for doing something well or winning a contest.

*A **medal** is given out to the winner at many sporting events.*

Microphone *noun*
A device used to make sounds louder.

*Debbie sings into the **microphone**, pretending to be a rock star.*

Minute *noun*
A period of time sixty seconds long.

*You can use a stopwatch to see how far you can run in a **minute**.*

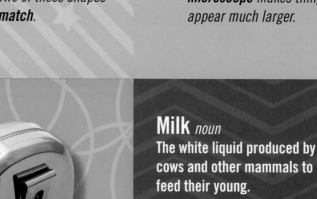

Mirror *noun*
A piece of glass with a shiny, reflective surface.

*The **mirror** is on a stand.*

Mittens *noun*
Warm hand coverings that protect your fingers in one part and have a separate pocket for your thumb.

*Chuckie is wearing green **mittens**.*

Miss *verb*
To feel sad that someone or something is not with you.

*Cosmo will **miss** Wanda if she is not around.*

Mix *verb*
To combine.

*When you **mix** white with a different color, you can create new shades of that color.*

Mistake *noun*
Something done wrong by accident.

*Oops! Carl made a **mistake** and forgot his shorts for gym class.*

Mom *noun*
A female parent.

*Timmy's **mom** has brown hair.*

Money *noun*
Special coins or paper used to buy things.

*This **money** is used in the United States.*

87

Monkey *noun*
A furry animal with a long, strong tail it uses to swing through trees and hang from branches.

*This animal is called a marmoset **monkey**.*

Mop *noun*
A long stick with a sponge or soft cloth used for cleaning attached to one end.

*Use a **mop** to keep floors clean and shiny.*

Motor *noun*
The part of a machine that helps all the other parts move.

*Patrick's boat has two **motors** in the back.*

MOTORS

Monster *noun*
A make-believe creature that is usually large and scary.

*This **monster** looks frightening!*

Month *noun*
A period of time about 30 days long.

*What **month** is your birthday in?*

Motorcycle *noun*
A vehicle that looks like a bicycle but has a powerful engine to make it move.

*Debbie and Donnie ride a **motorcycle**.*

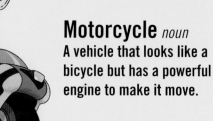

Mouse *noun*
A small, furry animal with a pointy nose, rounded ears, and a long tail.

*This **mouse** would love a piece of cheese to eat.*

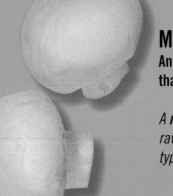

Mushroom *noun*
An umbrella-shaped fungus that grows in dirt.

*A **mushroom** can be eaten raw or cooked, but some types are poisonous.*

Movie *noun*
A story told with moving pictures.

*Marianne is making a **movie** of her family's adventures.*

Music *noun*
Sound produced by playing notes one after the other.

Music is written down using special symbols called musical notes.

Mud *noun*
Wet dirt.

*Goddard steps in a puddle of **mud**.*

Mystery *noun*
Something unusual that cannot be explained.

*It is a **mystery** what Jimmy's new invention is.*

Nn

Nail *noun*
A small, metal spike used to connect two pieces of wood or other materials.

*The bottom end of a **nail** is very sharp.*

Napkin *noun*
A piece of soft paper or fabric used to keep your face and hands clean during meals.

*This **napkin** holds the silverware in place.*

Nail polish *noun*
A special kind of paint used to color fingernails and toenails.

*Ginger paints her toenails with her favorite color of **nail polish**.*

Narrow *adjective*
Having a small width; skinny. *Narrow* is the opposite of *wide*.

*Compared to the snowboard, these skis are **narrow**.*

Name *noun*
A word used to identify something.

*Gary is the **name** of SpongeBob's pet snail.*

GARY

Near *preposition*
Close by. *Near* is the opposite of *far*.

*Eliza, Donnie, and Darwin are very **near** the edge of the cliff.*

Nap *verb*
To sleep for only a short amount of time.

*Patrick likes to **nap**.*

Necklace *noun*
A piece of jewelry worn around the neck.

*Angelica wears a lei, a special **necklace** made out of flowers.*

Need *verb*
To have to have something because you cannot do without it.

*Cosmo and Wanda **need** their wands to perform magic.*

Net *noun*
String or cords woven together to hold or catch things.

*SpongeBob is about to catch a jellyfish with his **net**.*

Neighbor *noun*
A person who lives close by.

*Darren is Ginger's **neighbor**.*

Never *adverb*
Not ever.

*You should **never** forget to wear your helmet when riding your bicycle.*

Nest *noun*
A home made by birds or other small animals to live in and raise their young.

*Donnie is careful not to drop the **nest** of eggs he has found.*

New *adjective*
Not used or known about before. *New* is the opposite of *old*.

*SpongeBob can't wait to try out his **new** surfboard.*

Newspaper *noun*
Big sheets of paper printed with words and pictures about the day's news.

*This **newspaper** reports on things that have happened in Retroville.*

RETROVILLE NEWS

POLITICAL RALLY IN RETROVILLE

DNA EXPANDS TO NEW OFFIC

Nice *adjective*
Kind or pleasing.

*Angelica was being very **nice** when she decided to buy flowers for her mom.*

Nine *adjective*
A number greater than eight and less than ten.

*There are **nine** fish.*

9

No *adverb*
What you say or write to disagree or refuse. *No* is the opposite of *yes*.

*Darwin was sad when Eliza said **no** to his idea.*

Nickname *noun*
A name used for a person in place of his or her given name.

*Did you know Chuckie is one **nickname** for a person whose real name is Charles?*

Notebook *noun*
A book with blank pages that you can write in.

*You use a **notebook** in school to write your lessons.*

SPONGEBOB BOATING 101

Night *noun*
The time of day when the sun goes down and the sky becomes dark.

*At **night**, you can often see the moon and stars.*

Noun *noun*
A word that names a person, place, or thing.

*A guitar is a thing, so the word guitar is a **noun**.*

Now *adverb*
Right at this moment. *Now* is the opposite of *later*.

*Angelica wants everyone to get off her chair right **now**!*

Nut *noun*
A seed, usually surrounded by a hard shell, that can be eaten.

*Before eating a **nut**, remove its shell.*

Nutcracker *noun*
A tool used to crack open the hard shell of a nut.

*A **nutcracker** can come in all kinds of designs, but they all perform the same job.*

Number *noun*
A value used for counting or to tell how many.

*Eight is the **number** that comes after seven.*

Nurse *noun*
A person trained to assist doctors and take care of sick or injured people.

*Wanda is dressed like a **nurse**.*

Oar *noun*
A long pole with a flat, broad end used to push water away to make a boat move.

*SpongeBob and Patrick each use an **oar** to row their boat.*

Oboe *noun*
A musical instrument you blow into while opening and closing air holes with buttons called keys.

*When you blow into an **oboe**, the reeds vibrate to create sound.*

Ocean *noun*
A large body of saltwater.

*There are lots of activities to do in the **ocean**.*

Off *preposition*
Not touching or on top of something else.

*Sam is **off** his skateboard.*

Office *noun*
A place where people work.

*SpongeBob has a large desk and a comfy chair in his **office**.*

Octopus *noun*
A sea animal with a soft, round body and eight long arms called *tentacles*.

*The words for more than one **octopus** are octopuses and octopi.*

Odd *adjective*
Having one left over after all others have been grouped together. *Odd* is the opposite of *even*.

*There is an **odd** number of friends here.*

Oil *noun*
A thick, greasy liquid pumped out of the ground and used for fuel and for helping things slide together smoothly; oil made from seeds and fruit is used for cooking.

*You can mix the **oil** on the left with vinegar to make salad dressing.*

Old *adjective*
Having existed for a long time. *Old* is the opposite of *new* or *young*.

*Grandma may be **old**, but she's still got enough energy for karate!*

On *preposition*
Touching something else, or above and held up by another thing.

*SpongeBob is riding **on** a jellyfish.*

One *adjective*
A number greater than zero and less than two.

*There is **one** star.*

Onion *noun*
A round vegetable made of many thin layers; onions have a strong smell and taste.

*The strong scent of a cut-up **onion** can make your eyes water.*

Open *verb*
To release from a closed position.

*Kimi is about to **open** her present.*

Opposite *noun*
Something that is completely different from something else.

*Asleep is the **opposite** of awake.*

ASLEEP

AWAKE

Orange *noun*
A round, orange-colored citrus fruit.

***Oranges** have lots of vitamin C.*

Ornament *noun*
An object used for decoration.

*These star-shaped **ornaments** are used to decorate Christmas trees.*

Outside *adverb*
On the outer side of something. *Outside* is the opposite of *inside*.

*Brrr! It's cold **outside** in the snow.*

Ostrich *noun*
A large bird with a very long neck and long legs.

*The **ostrich** can run very fast but cannot fly.*

Owl *noun*
A bird with a big, round head and large eyes that mostly hunts at night and sleeps during the day.

*This **owl** has just spotted his prey.*

Out *preposition*
On the outside of something. *Out* is the opposite of *in*.

*This red crayon has been taken **out** of the box.*

Oyster *noun*
A shellfish you can eat that also produces pearls.

*If you find a pearl inside an **oyster**, you are very lucky!*

Pack *verb*

To put belongings in a suitcase, box, or other container in order to take or send them somewhere.

*Before going on vacation, you **pack** a suitcase.*

Paintbrush *noun*

A brush used for painting.

*A large **paintbrush** is useful for painting a door or table.*

P p

Package *noun*

A box or thick envelope containing things that have been packed inside.

*These **packages** are too heavy to carry.*

Pajamas *noun*

Clothes worn for sleeping.

*Macie is still wearing her **pajamas** because she is home sick.*

Paint *verb*

To cover a surface with color for decoration or to make a picture.

*When SpongeBob decides to **paint**, he likes to make a picture of himself.*

Panda *noun*

A large animal with black and white fur that looks similar to a bear.

*A **panda** likes to eat bamboo leaves.*

Pants *noun*
A piece of clothing that slips over each leg separately and is pulled up to the waist.

*Francis wears a chain on his **pants**.*

Pp

Pattern *noun*
A design that repeats itself.

*The gift wrap on this present has a holiday **pattern**.*

Parade *noun*
A large group of people marching, dancing, or playing musical instruments as they move along a street.

*Out in the wild, Eliza and her friends put on their own **parade**.*

Pay *verb*
To give money to buy something.

*Angelica had to **pay** for lots of things when she went shopping.*

Park *noun*
An outdoor area where people can play, walk through gardens, or relax.

*SpongeBob finds butterflies at the **park**.*

Party *noun*
An event in which people gather to celebrate something and often talk, eat, and play games or dance.

*Hats and noisemakers add to the excitement of a **party**.*

Pea *noun*
A small, round vegetable that grows in a pod.

*You will find more than one **pea** when you open a pea pod.*

Peach *noun*
A juicy fruit with a soft, fuzzy skin.

*A **peach** has a hard pit in the middle that contains the seed.*

Pear *noun*
A firm, juicy fruit wide at the bottom and narrow at the top.

*Do not pick a **pear** until it is ripe or it will be too hard to eat.*

Peel *verb*
To take the skin or outside covering off something.

*You must **peel** bananas to eat the fruit inside.*

Pen *noun*
A tool filled with ink and used for writing.

*This **pen** writes with red ink.*

Pencil *noun*
A tool, made of wood and filled with graphite, that is used for writing and drawing.

*It is very unusual to see a **pencil** with wings, but not when Cosmo and Wanda are around!*

Penguin *noun*
A bird that cannot fly but can swim very fast in the icy-cold waters near where it lives.

*The **penguin** waddles when it walks.*

Pepper *noun*
A vegetable that comes in many colors and flavors.

***Pepper** is also a spice that flavors food!*

THE VEGETABLE

THE SPICE

99

Pet *noun*
A tame animal cared for by the people it lives with.

*Darwin is more than Eliza's **pet**. He is her friend!*

Picnic basket *noun*
A container used to hold food and supplies for a picnic.

*A **picnic basket** is light to carry but very strong.*

Picture *noun*
A drawing or painting hung up or displayed for decoration.

*This **picture** has a beautiful gold frame.*

Piano *noun*
A musical instrument with a keyboard you touch with your fingers to make the wires inside create sounds.

*When you play a **piano**, you can change the sound of the notes by pushing the pedals.*

Pie *noun*
A food made out of a pastry crust filled with fruit or meat and vegetables.

*This delicious **pie** is cooling on a plate.*

Picnic *noun*
A meal eaten outdoors.

*What's Donnie eating at the **picnic**?*

Pigeon *noun*
A bird with a large body and a small head that often lives in cities.

*Arnold doesn't even notice the **pigeon** right behind him.*

Piggy bank *noun*

A container, often shaped like a pig, for storing money.

*To get money out of a **piggy bank**, you sometimes have to break it open.*

Pilot *noun*

A person who flies planes or helicopters.

*Fasten your seat belts—this **pilot** is ready for takeoff!*

Piñata *noun*

A hanging party decoration that blindfolded people take turns trying to break open.

*At a celebration, you hit a **piñata** with a stick until candy and confetti fall out.*

Pile *noun*

A stack of things.

*A **pile** of oranges fell on top of Helga.*

Pineapple *noun*

A large fruit with a hard, prickly skin.

*When you cut into a **pineapple**, the juicy yellow fruit inside smells so good.*

Pillow *noun*

A sealed fabric bag, stuffed with feathers or other soft filling, for resting your head on.

*Grab your **pillow**, Patrick— it's time for bed!*

Ping-Pong *noun*

A game in which two people use small, round paddles to hit a small ball back and forth across a table.

***Ping-Pong** is also called table tennis.*

Pirate *noun*

A person who uses a ship to rob people on other ships.

*SpongeBob pretends to be a **pirate**.*

Playground *noun*

An outdoor area where children can play.

*A slide is just one of the things you can play on at a **playground**.*

Plan *noun*

An idea for how to do something.

*It looks like Plankton is making a **plan** to trick SpongeBob and his friends.*

Point *verb*

To aim at something in order to call attention to it.

*Sometimes it's rude to **point** but not when you see a ghost. Run!*

Planet *noun*

An enormous ball of rock, metal, and gas that travels around a star.

*We live on the **planet** Earth.*

Police officer *noun*

A person trained to protect people and help stop or solve crimes.

*While on the job, a **police officer** often wears a special uniform.*

Plate *noun*

A flat, round dish used for holding food.

*Tommy has a **plate** of cookies for Santa.*

FOR SANTA

Polka dots *noun*

A pattern of dots against a background of a different color.

*This blue egg is covered with **polka dots**.*

Pom-pom *noun*
A ball of fluffy material cheerleaders and fans wave and shake during sports games.

*Pearl cheers and waves her red **pom-poms.** Go, team!*

Pool *noun*
A game played by using a long stick to knock balls on a table into holes in its sides and corners.

*In **pool**, you score points by hitting the balls into pockets.*

Pony *noun*
A small horse.

*This little **pony** has a blond mane.*

Potato *noun*
A vegetable with brown or reddish skin and white insides.

*When a **potato** is baked, its insides become soft and fluffy.*

Practice *verb*
To repeat something so you can become good or better at it.

*Sam **practices** on his skateboard.*

Ponytail *noun*
Hair tied back into a single bunch.

*Cindy ties her hair back in a **ponytail** to keep it neat.*

Present *noun*
Something you give to somebody for a special reason, or because you like that person.

*Susie loves her new **present**.*

Pretend *verb*
To do or say something that is make-believe.

*Angelica likes to **pretend** to be a superhero like her doll.*

Puck *noun*
A circular disk hockey players try to hit into a goal.

*When a **puck** is hit with a hockey stick, it flies across the ice very fast.*

Puddle *noun*
A small patch of water.

*Timmy steps in a **puddle**.*

Pretty *adjective*
Nice to look at.

*Courtney has a **pretty** new dress.*

Proud *adjective*
Very pleased about something that you have or that you said or did.

*Jimmy is **proud** of all his ideas and inventions.*

Puffin *noun*
A black bird with a large, colored beak.

*A **puffin** likes to feed on fish.*

Pull *verb*

To move something toward you. *Pull* is the opposite of *push*.

This fishing hook is going to **pull** SpongeBob right out of the water.

Push *verb*

To move something away from you. *Push* is the opposite of *pull*.

Patrick loves to **push** the grocery cart.

Puppet *noun*

A doll you move around with your hands or with strings.

Kimi likes to pretend her **puppet** can talk.

Qq

Question *noun*

Words asked to find out something you want to know.

To ask a **question** in school, raise your hand like SpongeBob.

Puppy *noun*

A young dog.

The **puppy** wants to play!

Quick *adjective*
Fast.

*SpongeBob is **quick** when he's running scared!*

Rabbit *noun*
A small, furry, hopping animal with long ears and a small, fuzzy tail.

*Many people keep a **rabbit** as a pet.*

Rr

Quiet *adjective*
Making very little or no noise. *Quiet* is the opposite of *loud*.

*It is never **quiet** when Vicky is around!*

Radio *noun*
A machine that receives electrical signals and gives off sounds so listeners can hear music or talking.

*Arnold likes to listen to music on his **radio**.*

Quilt *noun*
A thick, soft blanket often made out of small pieces of fabric sewn together.

*The **quilt** on this bed has shapes on it.*

Quiver *verb*
To shake a little.

*Cosmo tries not to **quiver** with fear at the thought of jumping off the diving board.*

Rain *noun*
Water that falls from clouds.

*Umbrellas protect you from **rain**.*

Rainbow *noun*
A band of colors that can sometimes be seen when light shines through rain or glass.

*Seeing a **rainbow** makes SpongeBob very happy.*

Raw *adjective*
Not cooked.

*Sushi is a Japanese dish made with **raw** fish.*

Rat *noun*
A small, furry animal with sharp teeth and a very long tail.

*A **rat** is larger than a mouse.*

Read *verb*
To look at words and understand their meaning.

*SpongeBob loves to **read**.*

Rattle *noun*
A baby's toy that makes noise when shaken.

*Tommy Pickles shakes his **rattle** to make music.*

Recorder *noun*
A musical instrument you blow into while covering finger holes.

*Many children learn to play the **recorder** at school.*

Rectangle *noun*
A shape with two long, straight sides and two shorter straight sides.

*This shape is a **rectangle**.*

Rhinoceros *noun*
A very large, thick-skinned animal with one or two horns on top of its nose.

*The **rhinoceros** can use its horns to defend itself.*

Referee *noun*
A person who makes sure the rules of a game are followed.

*As the game **referee**, SpongeBob makes sure everyone plays fair!*

PEA, BEE, TEA, FLEA, ME!

Rhyme *verb*
To group words that end with the same sound, such as *beak* and *leak*.

*SpongeBob **rhymes** words with sea.*

Refrigerator *noun*
A machine that keeps food cold.

*This **refrigerator** is full of fresh food and drink.*

Relax *verb*
To rest or become calm.

*Cat wants to **relax**, but all Dog wants to do is talk!*

Ribbon *noun*
An award given when you do good work or perform well.

*The color of a **ribbon** may show what place someone finished in a competition; blue is often used for first place.*

108

Ride *noun*
To be moved or brought somewhere in a vehicle.

*Captain SquarePants thinks there's nothing better than to **ride** in a boat.*

Right *adjective*
The side or direction opposite the left. *Right* is the opposite of *left*.

*The arrow is pointing to the **right** side of this page.*

Ring *noun*
A piece of jewelry worn around a finger.

*This **ring** has a diamond in it.*

Roar *noun*
A loud, long sound made by animals, machines, rushing water, and so on.

*Donnie lets out a loud **roar**.*

Robot *noun*
A machine that can be made to do jobs easier or faster than people can do them.

*This **robot** throws snowballs super fast!*

Rock *noun*
A hard, heavy piece of stone.

*Eliza tells Darwin they should hide behind the **rock**.*

Rocket *noun*
A very fast vehicle that takes astronauts or equipment into outer space.

*Jimmy uses his **rocket** to fly into space.*

Rose *noun*
A flower with prickly thorns and bright, often sweet-smelling petals.

*Cosmo has a box of candy and **roses** for Wanda.*

Rodeo *noun*
A competition where cowboys and cowgirls on horses perform tasks and tricks.

*Susie is all dressed up for her first visit to the **rodeo**.*

Rowboat *noun*
A small boat moved by pulling its oars so they push water away.

*Donnie almost falls out of the **rowboat** when he spots a crocodile.*

Rope *noun*
A cord made of very strong fibers woven tightly together.

*Is that a superhero swinging on that **rope**? No, it's Jimmy Neutron!*

Rug *noun*
A heavy piece of fabric used to cover a floor.

*CatDog have a big circular **rug** in their living room.*

Ruler *noun*
A flat tool with straight edges used to measure and draw straight lines.

*This L-shaped **ruler** helps you draw corners.*

Run *verb*
To go quickly by moving your legs very fast.

*SpongeBob likes to **run** for excercise.*

Saddle *noun*
A special seat for riding a horse.

*Tommy sits on the **saddle**.*

Ss

Safe *adjective*
Not in danger; protected.

*To be **safe**, have a life preserver nearby when you go on a boat.*

Sad *adjective*
Unhappy. *Sad* is the opposite of *happy*.

*Squidward looks **sad** to have a hook on his tentacle.*

Salad *noun*
Fresh, uncooked fruits or vegetables, or both, mixed together.

*This tasty **salad** is served in a big bowl.*

Salt *noun*
White, grainy crystals used to flavor food.

Salt comes from salt mines or from the sea.

Sandbox *noun*
A container of sand that you can play in.

Someone left a toy behind in the *sandbox.*

Same *adjective*
Alike or matching.

*Lil is wearing the **same** style of snowsuit as Phil.*

Sand *noun*
Tiny grains of rock that cover the ground on a beach or in a desert.

*One of SpongeBob and Patrick's favorite things to do at the beach is bury each other in **sand**.*

Saxophone *noun*
A musical instrument made of a curved metal tube you blow air into while opening and closing air holes with buttons called keys.

*A **saxophone** is popular for playing the type of music known as jazz.*

Scale *noun*
A device that measures weight or length.

*When you step on a **scale**, it shows you how much your body weighs.*

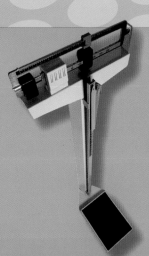

Scare *verb*
To frighten.

*These bullies are always trying to **scare** CatDog.*

Scarecrow *noun*
A figure made to look like a person to scare birds away so they won't eat crops.

*When a **scarecrow** is standing in a farmer's field, birds think it's a real person!*

Scarf *noun*
A long, soft piece of fabric worn around the neck.

*This **scarf** is so long, Phil and Lil have tangled themselves up in it!*

School *noun*
A place where people go to learn.

*What grade are you in at **school**?*

School bus *noun*
A vehicle that takes students to and from school or school sports events and on field trips.

*This is the **school bus** that travels to and from Jimmy Neutron's school each day.*

Scientist *noun*
A person who studies science and often works in a laboratory.

*A **scientist** often performs experiments.*

Scissors *noun*
A tool with two sharp edges used to cut paper and fabric.

*These **scissors** have very pointy ends.*

Screwdriver *noun*
A tool to help you turn screws tightly.

*A **screwdriver** is the perfect tool for putting up shelves.*

Scold *verb*
To speak to somone angrily because they have done something wrong.

*Cat **scolds** Dog for being messy.*

Scooter *noun*
A vehicle with a handle, a board to stand on, two wheels, and sometimes an engine.

*Reggie rides a **scooter**.*

Sea *noun*
A large body of saltwater.

*SpongeBob and Patrick take a clamshell ride in the **sea**.*

Seagull *noun*
A white-and-gray bird that lives near the sea.

***Seagulls** swoop down and catch fish that jump out of the water.*

Sea star noun

A star-shaped sea creature with a spiny body and many (often five) arms.

Sea stars live on the ocean floor.

Sea horse noun

A small sea animal with a long, curled tail and a head that looks like a horse's.

Yeehaw! Riding a sea horse is an adventure!

Secret noun

Something only you or a few people know and that you don't tell to anyone else.

Sandy wonders whether to tell SpongeBob and Patrick her secret.

Sea lion noun

A large sea animal with a long neck, a round body covered in smooth fur, and flippers on its sides.

A sea lion barks when it is hungry!

See verb

To use your eyes to look at something.

With these binoculars, SpongeBob can see things that are far away.

Season noun

A time of the year when certain weather is expected.

If you see snowflakes it is probably the winter season.

SEEDS

Seed noun

The part of a plant that can be put into the ground or a pot of soil to grow a new plant.

The melon has lots of seeds inside.

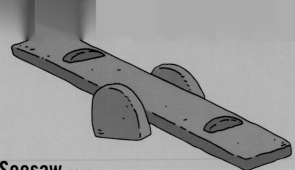

Seesaw *noun*
A balanced board on which two people sit at opposite ends and take turns pushing up off the ground.

*The **seesaw** is a toy you can find at the playground.*

Seven *adjective*
A number greater than six and less than eight.

7

*There are **seven** beans.*

Selfish *adjective*
Caring only about yourself.

*Cat thinks Dog is **selfish** to not share the doll.*

Shape *noun*
The outline of a thing's form.

*The **shape** of this sea sponge is a heart.*

Shark *noun*
A big fish with rows of large, very sharp teeth.

*The **shark** lives in saltwater.*

Send *verb*
To make something or someone go from one place to another.

*SpongeBob **sends** this ball flying through the air.*

Sharp *adjective*
Having a pointed end or edge that can cut or slice.

*This **sharp** blade can cut through metal.*

116

Shave *verb*
To use a razor or shaver to remove body hair.

*It's probably not a good idea for Patrick to **shave** his eyebrows!*

Short *adjective*
Having a small amount of time or space between beginning and end or between top and bottom. *Short* is the opposite of *long* or *tall*.

*Babies are **short**, so when they sit at a table with other people they need a high chair.*

Sheep *noun*
A large animal with a woolly coat that is often shaved off to use as fabric.

*People make yarn out of wool cut from a **sheep**.*

Shovel *noun*
A tool used for digging.

*A **shovel** is a good tool for digging in the garden.*

Shell *noun*
A hard, protective covering some creatures have on their bodies or that covers their eggs.

*Sandy is trying to get out of the clam's **shell**.*

Shower *noun*
A way of cleaning yourself by standing under a spray of water.

*When Dog takes a **shower**, Cat prefers to not get wet.*

Shoes *noun*
Foot coverings, usually made with leather or fabric, that have a hard surface on the bottom.

*Gary looks at his **shoes** to check that his laces are still tied.*

117

Shut *verb*
To close.

Darwin **shuts** his eyes as he jumps from a tree.

Silly *adjective*
Funny or full of nonsense.

Plankton is trying to look tough but he just looks **silly**.

Sidewalk *noun*
A raised walkway that runs alongside a road.

A crossing guard helps you safely reach the **sidewalk** on the opposite side of the street.

STOP

Sing *verb*
To use your voice to make music.

Susie **sings** a song.

Sight *noun*
The ability to see things.

These glasses make SpongeBob's **sight** much better.

Sink *noun*
A container with a faucet attached to it for holding or collecting water.

This **sink** is shaped like a duck.

Siren *noun*
A device that makes a warning sound and flashing lights.

*You might see a **siren** on a police car or an ambulance.*

Ski *verb*
To push yourself over snow by wearing long, narrow boards on your feet and using poles to help guide you.

*Learning to **ski** is not as easy as it looks!*

Six *adjective*
A number greater than five and less than seven.

*There are **six** flowers.*

Skateboard *noun*
A board on four wheels you stand and balance on as it moves along a hard surface.

*Angelica rides a **skateboard**.*

Skip *verb*
To move forward by hopping from one foot to the other.

*Tommy has learned how to **skip**.*

Skeleton *noun*
The structure of all the bones inside your body.

*The human **skeleton** has 206 bones.*

Skirt *noun*
A piece of clothing that hangs freely from the waist down.

*When he dances, Patrick wears a grass **skirt**.*

Sky noun
All the air far above the earth.

*Sometimes the **sky** looks blue and is full of fluffy white clouds.*

Slide verb
To move quickly and easily over a surface.

*At the playground, the Rugrats like to **slide**.*

Sled noun
A flat vehicle you sit on to ride through snow.

*Jimmy and Carl go fast on this **sled**.*

Sleep verb
To close your eyes and become unaware in order to rest your mind and body.

*Patrick doesn't need a bed to **sleep**—he can do it anywhere!*

Slow adjective
Not quick. *Slow* is the opposite of *fast*.

*Gary the snail is very **slow**, so SpongeBob waits for him.*

Smell verb
To use your nose to pick up scents or odors.

*Susie **smells** the flowers.*

Smile *verb*
To make a happy face by curving up the corners of your mouth.

*SpongeBob **smiles** when he is happy.*

Snowboard *noun*
A board you balance on as you slide down a snowy surface.

*Riding a **snowboard** is similar to surfing, but you travel on snow instead of waves.*

Snake *noun*
A long, narrow reptile with no legs that moves by sliding its body along the ground.

*This **snake** is called a cobra.*

Snowman *noun*
A figure made of snow.

*This **snowman** wears a tall hat.*

Snorkel *verb*
To swim underwater using a breathing tube and a mask.

*When you **snorkel**, you can see fish swim underwater.*

Soccer *noun*
A game played by two teams that each try to kick a ball into the other team's goal.

*Chuckie and Tommy play a game of **soccer**.*

Snow *noun*
White, powdery flakes that form when water vapor falls from clouds during cold weather.

*Kimi made a snowball out of the **snow**.*

Socks *noun*
Soft coverings for your feet.

*Libby is wearing green **socks**.*

Sometimes *adverb*
Now and then, but not always.

*Patrick **sometimes** tries to fit into SpongeBob's square pants. But it never works!*

Soft *adjective*
Fine to the touch. **Soft** is the opposite of *hard*.

*The fur trim on Donnie's coat feels very **soft**.*

Song *noun*
Music that may include words.

*Gary plays a **song** on his record player.*

Space *noun*
The area all around Earth that stars, planets, and other bodies move through.

*Plankton is ready for his trip into **space**.*

Sombrero *noun*
A wide-brimmed hat popular in some Latin cultures.

*Wearing a **sombrero** keeps the sun off your face.*

Spatula *noun*
A cooking tool with a flat end used for lifting or turning food.

*Tito cooked this hamburger on both sides by flipping it with his **spatula**.*

Spin *verb*
To turn around over and over again.

*The babies **spin** their tops.*

Spider *noun*
A small creature with eight legs.

*This furry **spider** has lots of eyes!*

Sponge *noun*
A piece of material that soaks water up and is often used for bathing or cleaning.

*If you spill a drink, a **sponge** can quickly soak it up.*

Spiderweb *noun*
Loosely woven patterns of silk that spiders spin to catch insects.

*This **spiderweb** spells out a special holiday message!*

Spoon *noun*
A tool for eating or serving food that has a long handle with a small, shallow bowl at one end.

*This wooden **spoon** is used to stir food while cooking.*

Sprinkler *noun*
An object used to spray water.

*Patrick would make a very good **sprinkler** for a garden!*

Star *noun*
A burning ball of gas that can be seen in the sky at night (except for the Sun, which is a star that we see in the daytime).

*A **star** is also the name of a shape that looks like one of these!*

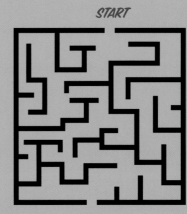

Square *noun*
A shape with four straight, equal sides.

*These wooden tiles are all shaped like **squares**.*

START

Start *verb*
To begin something. *Start* is the opposite of *end*.

*To complete the maze you must **start** at the top.*

END

Squash *noun*
A vegetable with a leathery rind and soft, fleshy insides.

*During Thanksgiving, people decorate their homes with different types of **squash**.*

Squirrel *noun*
A small, furry animal with a long, bushy tail.

*Sandy is no ordinary **squirrel**.*

State *noun*
One of the fifty areas of land the United States is divided into.

*What **state** do you live in?*

Statue *noun*
A figure sculpted, carved, or cast in a material such as clay or metal to look like a person or thing.

*The **Statue** of Liberty is in New York City.*

Stethoscope *noun*
A tool doctors use to listen to your heartbeat and other sounds inside your body.

*A doctor uses a **stethoscope** by putting the earpiece in his or her ears and the disk over your chest.*

Steer *verb*
To guide something in the direction you want it to go.

*SpongeBob uses the wheel to **steer** the boat.*

Stocking *noun*
A bag for holding gifts that is shaped like a large sock.

*Some people hang up a **stocking** at Christmas.*

Stem *noun*
The long, thin part of a flower that petals and leaves are attached to.

*Dil holds the flower by its **stem**.*

Stop *verb*
To come or bring to an end.

*This sign tells drivers to **stop**.*

Strawberry *noun*
A small, red fruit that grows on a small plant.

*When a **strawberry** is plump and red, it's ripe and ready to be eaten!*

Strong *adjective*
Having a lot of strength or power. **Strong** is the opposite of *weak*.

*Sandy can lift the heavy weight because she is **strong**.*

Stretch *verb*
To lengthen something.

*Cat and Dog **stretch** in different directions.*

Student *noun*
A person learning new things.

*Patrick is excited to be a **student**.*

Stripe *noun*
A long, narrow band with a different color than its background.

*This shirt has lots of **stripes**.*

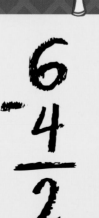

Subtract *verb*
To take away. **Subtract** is the opposite of *add*.

*When you **subtract** four from six, you get two.*

Suitcase *noun*
A container with handles that is used to carry belongings when you travel.

*Plankton carries a **suitcase** he packed for a trip.*

Sunglasses *noun*
Darkened lenses worn to protect your eyes from sunlight.

***Sunglasses** make everything look a little darker.*

Sunscreen *noun*
A cream or lotion you put on your body to protect it from the sun's rays.

*It's very important to put **sunscreen** on regularly to keep your skin from burning.*

sun screen

*

Sum *noun*
The amount you get when you add numbers together.

*When you add 3 plus 3, the **sum** is 6.*

$$\begin{array}{r} 3 \\ +\,3 \\ \hline 6 \end{array}$$

Surf *verb*
To balance on a board and ride on top of waves in the ocean.

*To **surf**, Sam uses his arms to help him balance.*

Sun *noun*
The bright yellow star that shines in the sky during the day.

*The **Sun** gives the Earth light and warmth.*

Swan *noun*
A large, white bird with a long neck.

*The **swan's** neck is shaped like the letter S.*

Sweep *verb*
To clear away dirt using a broom or brush.

*It's better to **sweep** with a real brush than to use Cosmo or Wanda.*

Sweet *adjective*
Tasting like sugar or honey.

*Cookies are a **sweet** treat.*

Swim *verb*
To glide through water by moving your arms and legs.

*SpongeBob **swims** on his surfboard.*

Sword *noun*
A weapon with a long, pointed blade.

*Sandy holds a fake wooden **sword** when she pretends to be a pirate.*

T-shirt *noun*
A shirt without a collar or buttons.

*Otto wears a yellow **T-shirt**.*

Tt

Table *noun*
A piece of furniture with a flat surface supported by legs.

*Cat and Dog sit at the **table** to eat a fish-and-bone sandwich.*

Tail *noun*
A part of an animal's body attached to its back that helps the animal balance or hold on to branches.

*When Spike wags his **tail**, it means he's happy to see you.*

Take *verb*
To bring along with you to another place.

*Carl is supposed to **take** his inhaler with him wherever he goes.*

Talk *verb*
To use your voice to speak.

Tucker uses his walkie-talkie to **talk** to his friend.

Tango *noun*
A kind of ballroom dance.

Helga dances the **tango** with Arnold.

Tall *adjective*
Having a large amount of space between top and bottom. *Tall* is the opposite of *short*.

Eliza uses a little help to photograph this **tall** giraffe.

Taste *verb*
To use your taste buds to recognize and enjoy the flavor of a food or drink.

Hoodsey **tastes** this chocolate snack.

Tambourine *noun*
A musical instrument shaped like the head of a drum that you shake or hit.

A **tambourine** is good for keeping rhythm during a song.

Taxicab *noun*
A car with a driver you pay to drive you somewhere.

To catch a **taxicab**, wave your hand and yell, "Taxi!"

Tea noun
A drink made from mixing water with flavorful leaves.

*You can add milk, sugar, or honey to **tea**.*

Telephone noun
A machine you use to talk to people who are not nearby.

*Talking on the **telephone** is almost as good as really being with your friends.*

Telescope noun
A tool you look through to see things that are far away.

*Plankton is using this **telescope** to see if he can spot SpongeBob in the distance.*

Teacher noun
A person trained to help people learn.

*Mr. Crocker is Timmy's **teacher**.*

Television noun
A machine that produces sound and moving pictures.

*Guess which **television** is old and which one is new?*

Teddy bear noun
A soft, cuddly toy that looks like a bear.

*The **teddy bear** has a red ribbon around its neck.*

Tell *verb*
To give information about something or someone.

*Winslow has a lot to **tell** Cat and Dog.*

Tentacle *noun*
A long, flexible part of the body on some animals used for feeling, grasping, or moving.

*Squidward trips over a **tentacle** as he tries to catch the football.*

Ten *adjective*
A number greater than nine and less than eleven.

*There are **ten** balloons.*

10

Tennis *noun*
A game played by two or four people who use rackets to hit a ball back and forth over a low net.

*This racket and ball are used in **tennis**.*

Test tube *noun*
A glass tube used in some science experiments.

*Scientists use **test tubes** to hold liquids when they do experiments.*

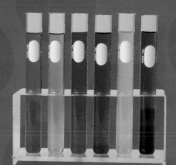

Thank *verb*
To tell people how much you like what they have done for you.

*When SpongeBob wants to **thank** someone, he sometimes has a unique way of doing it!*

Thermometer *noun*
A tool that measures weather or body temperature.

*If you are sick, a **thermometer** will tell you if you have a fever.*

Thoughtful *adjective*
Thinking about other people and doing things for others in a caring way.

*It was **thoughtful** of Arnold to buy flowers for Grandma.*

Thread *noun*
A very thin string of cord used for sewing.

*Dil is making a popcorn garland by stringing popcorn with **thread**.*

Think *verb*
To use your mind to consider ideas.

*Hugh **thinks** about what to eat for lunch.*

Thirsty *adjective*
Feeling the need to drink.

*SpongeBob is **thirsty**.*

Three *adjective*
A number greater than two and less than four.

*There are **three** cans of paint.*

3

Throne noun
A chair that kings and queens sit on during special occasions.

*Plankton likes to use this chair as his **throne**.*

Tickle verb
To use your fingers to touch people's skin in a way that feels nice, or that feels funny and makes them laugh.

*Goddard likes it when Jimmy **tickles** his tummy.*

Throw verb
To send something through the air with a motion of your arm and hand.

*Arnold and Gerald **throw** toy airplanes into the air.*

Tie verb
To fasten or hold together as with a cord or string.

*When SpongeBob plays golf, he manages to **tie** himself in a knot!*

Ticket noun
A piece of paper that shows the holder has paid for something.

*You must show your **ticket** before entering the movie theater.*

Tiger noun
A very large wild cat with orange fur with black stripes.

Tigers are the biggest cats in the world.

Tire noun
A hoop of thick rubber fitted around a wheel.

*Cars have four **tires**.*

Tissue noun
Soft paper used as a handkerchief or towel.

*Achoo! Grab a **tissue** when you need to blow your nose.*

Toboggan noun
A long sled used for traveling through snow.

*The Rugrats are traveling fast on this Reptar **toboggan**.*

Toad noun
An amphibian related to the frog but bigger and with rougher, drier skin.

*The **toad** is known for having warts all over its body.*

Today noun
The day that it is right now.

***Today** Plankton hopes to serve his only dish, Chumbalaya!*

CHUM BUCKET

today's special

CHUM-Balaya!

Toast noun
Sliced bread that is heated and browned.

*People often eat **toast** with butter for breakfast.*

Together adverb
Gathered in a single group.

*SpongeBob and Patrick love to be **together**.*

Toilet *noun*
A chair-shaped bowl with a seat connected to a drain that flushes away body waste.

*Poor Plankton is being flushed down the **toilet!***

Tomato *noun*
A round, red fruit often served in salads.

*Many people think the **tomato** is a vegetable, but it's actually a fruit!*

Tongue *noun*
The fleshy organ in your mouth that helps you taste, chew, swallow, and speak.

*Jimmy's invention makes him act silly and stick out his **tongue**.*

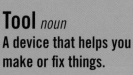

Tool *noun*
A device that helps you make or fix things.

*Whichever **tool** you need, SpongeBob has it in his toolbox or on his tool belt.*

Toothbrush *noun*
A small brush you use to clean your teeth.

*Patrick has dazzling teeth, because he always remembers to use his **toothbrush** after every meal.*

Toothpaste *noun*
A paste used on toothbrushes that helps clean your teeth.

***Toothpaste** often comes in a tube.*

toothpaste

Touch *verb*
To feel something with a part of your body.

*Eliza **touches** the spider's furry leg.*

Train *noun*
A line of railroad cars attached to each other that travels on tracks.

*Choo choo! Here comes the **train!***

Tower *noun*
A very tall and narrow building or other structure.

*The famous Eiffel **tower** is in Paris, France.*

Trash can *noun*
A container for holding garbage.

*CatDog hide in the **trash can** so Shriek cannot find them.*

Toy *noun*
Something you play with.

*This truck is not real; it is just a **toy**.*

Travel *verb*
To go somewhere.

*When you **travel** to another country, you may need to take a passport with you.*

PASSPORT

Treasure chest *noun*
A container where precious or important things are stored.

*This **treasure chest** is overflowing with gold coins.*

Treat *noun*
Something special.

*Gingerbread cookies are a holiday **treat**.*

Tricycle *noun*
A small three-wheeled bicycle for young children.

*SpongeBob rides a **tricycle**.*

Tree *noun*
A large plant with a trunk and branches.

*The **tree** is covered with snow.*

Trip *noun*
A visit to another place.

*Timmy's dad dressed in cool clothes for his **trip** to the beach.*

Triangle *noun*
A shape with three straight sides.

*This musical instrument is called a **triangle** because of its shape.*

Trombone *noun*
A musical instrument you blow into while sliding a part of it back and forth.

*The **trombone** is often played in marching bands.*

Trophy *noun*
A prize you are given when you perform well in a contest.

*A cup like this is a popular sporting **trophy**.*

Try *verb*
To make an effort to do something.

*Gerald wants to **try** playing pool.*

Truck *noun*
A large vehicle with a strong engine and four or more wheels that is used to carry or tow things.

*This **truck** has big tires.*

Tuba *noun*
A very large, curving musical instrument you play by blowing into a mouthpiece and pressing buttons called keys.

*A **tuba** has a very low, deep sound.*

True *adjective*
Real or actual.

*It is **true** that sometimes Donnie behaves like a wild animal.*

Trumpet *noun*
A musical instrument you blow into while opening and closing air holes with buttons called keys.

*The **trumpet** looks very easy to play, but it takes much practice, just like any other instrument.*

Tulip *noun*
A cup-shaped flower with a long stem.

*Angelica performs a dance with a pink **tulip** between her teeth.*

Turn *verb*
To move your body or an object around to face a different direction.

*Goddard **turns** his head to look over his shoulder.*

12

Twelve *adjective*
A number greater than eleven and less than thirteen.

*There are **twelve** balls.*

Turtle *noun*
An animal with a hard shell covering its soft body.

*A sea **turtle** will lay its eggs in the sand and then bury them to keep them warm and safe.*

Twin *noun*
A person with the same parents as someone else and born at the same time.

*Phil and Lil are **twins**.*

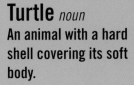

Tweezers *noun*
A tool used for picking up very small things.

***Tweezers** are used by squeezing the two parts around the object you want to pick up.*

2

Two *adjective*
A number greater than one and less than three.

*There are **two** ice skates.*

Uu

Ugly *adjective*
Unpleasant looking; not nice to look at.

*SpongeBob is making an **ugly** face.*

Umpire *noun*
A person who makes sure the rules of a game are followed.

*In some sports, an **umpire** is called a referee.*

Ukelele *noun*
A small guitar with four strings.

*SpongeBob plays the **ukelele**.*

Under *preposition*
Lower than or beneath something else.

*SpongeBob is trapped **under** Patrick.*

Umbrella *noun*
A covering you hold over your head with a handle to protect yourself from rain or sun.

*Wanda turned into a pink **umbrella**.*

Underground *adverb*
Beneath the ground.

*Many small creatures live **underground**, like these worms Phil found.*

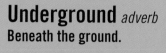

Underwear *noun*

The clothing you wear underneath all your other clothes.

*Look! You can see SpongeBob's **underwear**.*

Unique *adjective*

Different from anything else.

*Everyone has a **unique** set of teeth.*

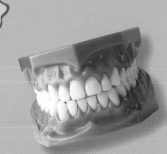

Unicycle *noun*

A cycle with only one wheel.

*You need good balance to ride a **unicycle**.*

University *noun*

A school where adults can study a subject.

*Plankton graduated from the **University** of Bikini Bottom with a diploma in EVIL!*

Uniform *noun*

A special outfit you wear to show you are part of a group or have a certain job.

*A police cap is part of a police officer's **uniform**.*

Unlucky *adjective*

Having bad things happen to you by chance. ***Unlucky*** is the opposite of *lucky*.

*It was **unlucky** for Helga to walk under Grandma's window.*

Unwind *verb*
To reverse the winding or twisting of something.

Kimi lets her toy **unwind** then watches it fly through the air.

Use *verb*
To put an object into service.

SpongeBob tries to **use** a jackhammer, but he is not doing it very well!

Up *adverb*
Going from a lower place to a higher place.

SpongeBob and Patrick jump **up** high.

Usual *adjective*
Happening often.

Grandma's **usual** breakfast is pancakes.

Upside down *adjective*
Flipped over so the bottom end is at the top and the top end is at the bottom.

SpongeBob is **upside down**.

Usually *adverb*
Most of the time.

Ginger **usually** talks on the phone with her friends at night.

Vacation *noun*
A period of time when you do not go to school or work.

*SpongeBob is ready for a **vacation**.*

V v

Vacant *adjective*
Empty.

*No one is sitting in this desk. It is **vacant**.*

Valentine *noun*
A card or gift sent on St. Valentine's Day; also, a person you like very much.

*Chuckie is happy that he received a special **valentine**.*

Vacuum cleaner *noun*
A machine that cleans by sucking dirt and dust up with a hose.

*SpongeBob has an extraordinary **vacuum cleaner** to suck up all the stray shells.*

Vase *noun*
A small container used for displaying cut flowers.

*A nice **vase** can make flowers look even prettier.*

Vehicle *noun*
An automobile that carries people and goods.

*This **vehicle** is called a bus.*

Video *noun*
A movie or other recording stored on a tape cassette.

*Twister is making a **video** of all his pals.*

Verb *noun*
A word used to show action.

*Catch is a **verb** because it describes an action.*

Video game *noun*
A game you can play on a television or computer screen.

*Sheen's busy with an Ultra Lord **video game**.*

Very *adverb*
Extremely, or by a large amount.

*SpongeBob has **very** big muscles after going to the gym.*

Vine *noun*
A plant with a stem that climbs or trails along the ground.

*Eliza and Darwin swing through the rain forest holding onto a **vine**.*

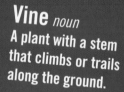

Vest *noun*
A sleeveless top usually worn over a shirt.

*This **vest** has a lot of pockets.*

144

Violin *noun*
A musical instrument you play by drawing a bow across its strings.

*When you play the **violin**, you rest it on your shoulder.*

Wake *verb*
To stop sleeping.

*Cat **wakes** up full of energy.*

Volleyball *noun*
A game played by two teams that hit a ball with their hands back and forth over a high net.

*Beach **volleyball** is a popular sport that uses a ball similar to this one.*

Walk *verb*
To move by repeatedly placing one foot in front of the other.

*Dash **walks** quickly down the street.*

Vulture *noun*
A large bird with a bald head and dark wings.

*A **vulture** circles the sky to look for food.*

Wall *noun*
An upright side of a room or building.

*Danny has the power to go through this **wall** when he goes ghost.*

Warm adjective
Between cold and hot.

It feels **warm** near the fire.

Wasp noun
A flying insect that is similar to a bee.

Like bees, **wasps** can sting!

Warthog noun
A wild hog with tusks that lives in Africa.

Warthogs get their name because they have warts on their faces!

Watch noun
A small clock worn on your wrist.

*Sam always wears a **watch,** even when he is riding his bike.*

Wash verb
To clean yourself or something else.

*To **wash**, Darwin scrubs himself with a brush.*

Water noun
A liquid that collects in rivers, lakes, and seas from rainfall and is also found in all living things.

*Would you like a glass of **water**?*

Water buffalo noun
A large animal with coarse hair and horns that lives in the wetlands of Asia.

The **water buffalo** is the largest type of buffalo.

Wax noun
An oily, solid substance that melts when it is heated.

Candles are made of **wax**.

Watermelon noun
A large fruit with a thick, green rind and red flesh inside that is full of dark seeds.

Watermelons are more than 90 percent water.

Weak adjective
Having little strength or power. *Weak* is the opposite of *strong*.

SpongeBob must be feeling very **weak** if he can barely lift these two stuffed animals.

Wave verb
To move your hand and arm from side to side to greet people or get their attention.

Carl **waves** hello to his friend Jimmy.

Wedding noun
An event in which two people marry.

At a **wedding**, people are served a special dessert called a wedding cake.

Weights *noun*
A heavy object lifted for exercise.

*This dumbell is a type of **weight**.*

Whale *noun*
A large animal that lives in the sea but breathes air and is not a fish.

*A **whale** is a mammal because it nurses its young with milk, just like a human.*

Well *adjective*
Healthy.

*Kimi feels **well** and is ready to start her day.*

Wheel *noun*
A round object that turns to make things move.

*Reggie pops a **wheel** in the air.*

Wet suit *noun*
Special clothing that keeps you warm when you are in the water.

*Surfers and scuba divers wear a **wet suit** in cold water.*

Wheelbarrow *noun*
A vehicle with a front wheel and handles used to carry small loads.

*This **wheelbarrow** is red.*

Wheelchair *noun*
A chair with four wheels designed to carry someone who cannot walk.

*To move this **wheelchair** while sitting in it, you turn the two largest wheels with your hands.*

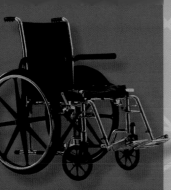

Whistle *noun*
A small device that makes a loud sound when you blow into it.

*Blowing a **whistle** is a good way to get people's attention.*

When *adverb*
A word used to ask questions about time, or to explain about time.

***When** does school let out? Three o'clock!*

Whisk *noun*
A cooking tool used to mix ingredients together.

*A **whisk** is good for mixing cake batter.*

Wide *adjective*
Having a great distance from one side to the other. ***Wide*** is the opposite of ***narrow***.

*Dil's mouth opens very **wide**!*

Whiskers *noun*
The long hairs that grow near the mouths of some animals.

*Cat has **whiskers**, Dog doesn't.*

Wife *noun*
A married woman.

*Wanda is Cosmo's **wife**.*

Wildebeest *noun*
A large animal that has a mane, a beard, and curved horns.

Wildebeests live in the wild.

Wing *noun*
The part of an animal's body that it flaps to help it fly.

*The bird spreads its **wings**.*

Window *noun*
A frame of glass in a wall, designed to let in light or air or both.

*Gerald and Arnold lean out the **window**.*

Wire *noun*
A long, thin piece of metal that electricity can pass through.

*Many electrical appliances in your house have **wires** in them.*

Wish *noun*
A strong desire for something.

*With godparents like Cosmo and Wanda, Timmy always gets his **wish**.*

WINDSHIELD →

Windshield *noun*
A large piece of glass that forms the front window of a vehicle.

*This car has a large **windshield**.*

Wolf *noun*
An animal related to dogs that lives in the wild.

*It is said that when a **wolf** sees the moon, it will howl.*

Wonderful *adjective*
Amazing and exciting or unusually good.

*SpongeBob is a **wonderful** friend.*

Woman *noun*
A grown-up girl.

*Marianne is a cheerful **woman**.*

Wombat *noun*
A small bear-like animal that lives in Australia.

***Wombats** look like bears but they are really related to kangaroos!*

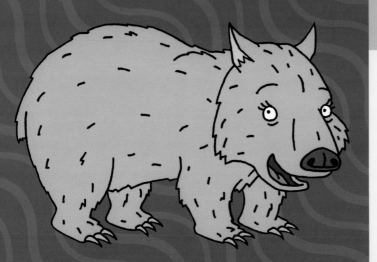

Wood *noun*
The hard material that comes from the trunks and branches of trees.

*Chopping blocks are made out of **wood**.*

Word *noun*
A group of letters that name something.

*Roach is not a **word** Plankton likes to be called!*

i am not a ROACH!

Work *verb*

To use energy and effort to do something.

*With his new invention, Jimmy doesn't have to **work** hard to rake leaves!*

Wow *interjection*

A word you say to show you are amazed or excited by something.

Wow! The Crimson Chin has the biggest chin ever!

Worm *noun*

A small animal that lives in soil and has a long, flexible body with no legs.

*When you find a **worm** in your garden, don't hurt it, because it's good for the soil.*

Wrap *verb*

To cover all over with paper or another material.

*There are always so many gifts to **wrap** during the holiday season.*

Worry *verb*

To think that something bad is going to happen or think about something bad that has happened.

*SpongeBob begins to **worry** that he left a Krabby Patty on the grill too long.*

Wreath *noun*

A ring of leaves or flowers.

*A **wreath** is a popular adornment for doors during the holidays.*

Wrench *noun*
A tool used for turning nuts and bolts.

*There is a **wrench** sized for every job.*

Wrestling *noun*
A sport or activity in which two people try to pin each other's shoulders to the ground.

Wrestling is a sport that gets Patrick all tied up in knots!

Write *verb*
To put words on paper or another writing surface or type them on a computer screen.

*Ginger thinks about what to **write** in her journal.*

X-ray *noun*
A picture taken to show the inside of your body.

*An **X-ray** can help doctors figure out why a person is sick.*

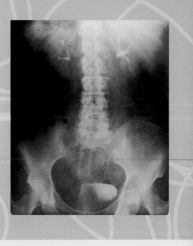

Xx

Xylophone *noun*
A musical instrument with bars of different sizes you hit with a small hammer called a mallet.

*The **xylophone** makes a sound similar to that of a bell.*

Yy

Yacht *noun*
A type of boat that people sail for fun.

*The **yacht** has wheels so it can be pulled when it's on land.*

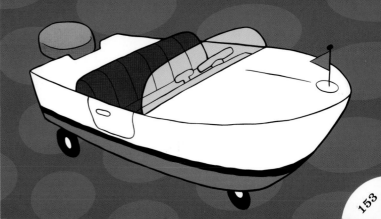

Yak *noun*
A large, hairy kind of ox that comes from Asia.

Yaks have good balance on snow and ice.

Year *noun*
A period of time 365 days long.

*SpongeBob thinks Krabby Patties are good to eat every month of the **year**.*

Yam *noun*
A vegetable that grows in the ground and is like a potato, except that it is orange inside and tastes sweet.

Yams are similar to sweet potatoes but they are not the same.

Yearn *verb*
To want something very much.

*Plankton always **yearns** for SpongeBob's Krabby Patties.*

Yawn *verb*
To open your mouth and let air in and out slowly.

*CatDog **yawn** when they are tired.*

Yell *verb*
To speak very loudly; to shout.

*Helga's often grumpy, so it doesn't take much to make her **yell**!*

Yes *adverb*
What you say or write to agree or accept. *Yes* is the opposite of *no.*

Darwin was so happy, he danced for joy when Eliza said **yes** to another adventure.

Yodel *verb*
To sing switching back and forth from high notes to low.

At the talent show, SpongeBob **yodels** a song.

Yesterday *noun*
The day before today.

Libby arranged to meet her friends **yesterday**.

Yoga *noun*
A system of exercises designed to help you become healthy and relaxed in mind and body.

SpongeBob is so good at **yoga** that he can even do this amazing pose!

Yippee *interjection*
A word you shout to express delight.

Cosmo was so happy his magic worked, he jumped in the air and shouted, **"Yippee!"**

Yolk *noun*
The yellow part of an egg.

These **yolks** are surrounded by the egg whites.

Young *adjective*
Having existed for a short time. *Young* is the opposite of *old*.

*Helga is a **young** girl.*

Zz

Zany *adjective*
Silly or goofy.

*Acting **zany** is one of SpongeBob's and Patrick's favorite things to do.*

Yo-yo *noun*
A toy that spins at the end of a length of string.

*There are lots of tricks you can do with a **yo-yo**.*

Zebra *noun*
A large animal related to the horse that has black and white markings.

*Eliza thinks a **zebra** looks a little like a patterned horse.*

Yucky *adjective*
Unpleasant or gross.

*Carl has a **yucky** surprise for Ginger!*

Zero *noun*
A number that means none.

*The number **zero** looks like this.*

n o p q r s t u v w x y z

Zigzag *noun*
A pattern that goes up and down in straight lines.

*This pattern is a **zigzag**.*

Zoo *noun*
A park where lots of animals of different kinds are kept so people can see and watch them.

*These are just some of the animals that can often be seen at a **zoo**.*

Zippy *adjective*
Fast and speedy; energetic.

*SpongeBob is feeling very **zippy** today!*

Zone *noun*
A particular place or area.

*Otto is going for a touchdown in the end **zone**.*

Zoom *verb*
To go very fast.

*SpongeBob **zooms** by in his racing car.*

Zucchini *noun*
A long, green vegetable that is a kind of squash.

Zucchini can be eaten raw or cooked.

157

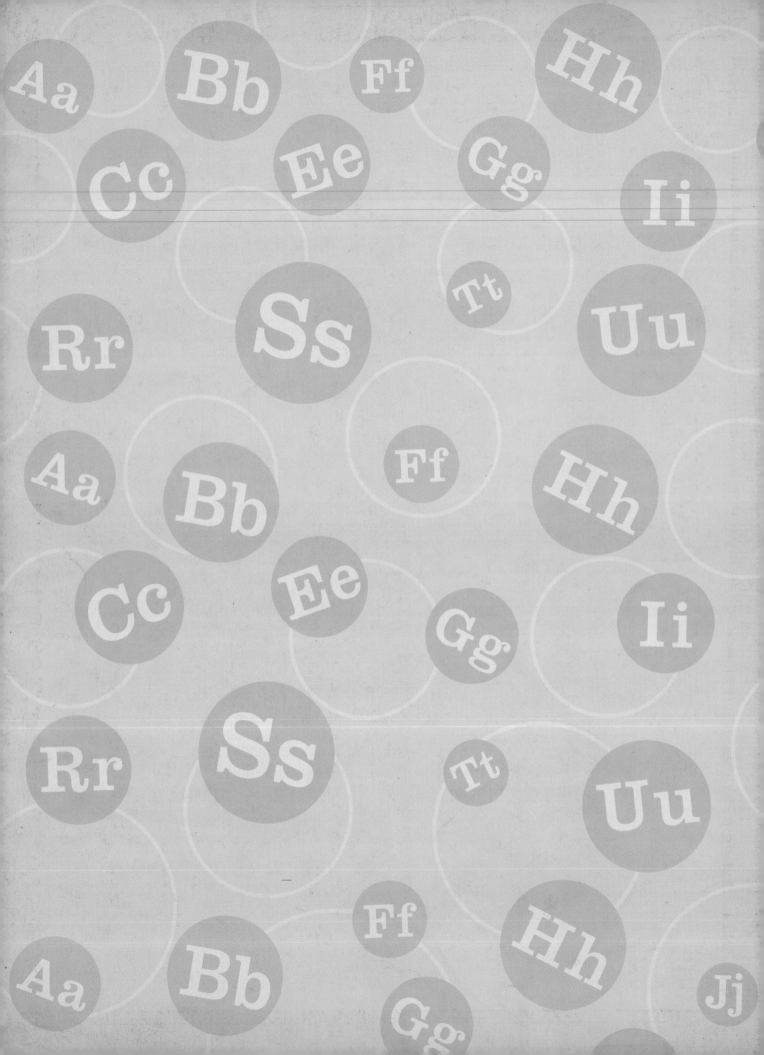